MW00800298

000   5000   6000   7000

LIGHTING

BEYOND EDISON

BRILLIANT RESIDENTIAL LIGHTING TECHNIQUES
in the Age of LEDs

Other Schiffer Books on Related Subjects:

Timeless Beauty: The Art of Louis Comfort Tiffany,
Charles Hosmer Morse Museum of Art,
ISBN 978-0-7643-5149-5

Art Deco Lighting,
Herb Millman and John Dwyer,
ISBN 978-0-7643-1357-8

Copyright © 2022 by Charles Pavarini III, J. Randall Tarasuk, and Mervyn Kaufman

Library of Congress Control Number: 2022932595

Designed by Christopher Bower
Cover design by Christopher Bower

Front cover: Photo by Pavarini Design
Back cover: Photo by Phillip Ennis

Type set in Avenir/ Minion Pro

ISBN: 978-0-7643-6500-3
Printed in India

Published by Schiffer Publishing, Ltd.
4880 Lower Valley Road
Atglen, PA 19310
Phone: (610) 593-1777; Fax: (610) 593-2002
Email: Info@schifferbooks.com
Web: www.schifferbooks.com

For our complete selection of fine books on this and related subjects, please visit our website at www.schifferbooks.com. You may also write for a free catalog.

Schiffer Publishing's titles are available at special discounts for bulk purchases for sales promotions or premiums. Special editions, including personalized covers, corporate imprints, and excerpts, can be created in large quantities for special needs. For more information, contact the publisher.

We are always looking for people to write books on new and related subjects. If you have an idea for a book, please contact us at proposals@schifferbooks.com.us at proposals@schifferbooks.com.

LIGHTING
BEYOND EDISON

BRILLIANT RESIDENTIAL LIGHTING TECHNIQUES
in the Age of LEDs

by **CHARLES PAVARINI III**
with
Mervyn Kaufman
and J. Randall Tarasuk

SCHIFFER PUBLISHING

4880 Lower Valley Road • Atglen, PA 19310

DEDICATION

This book is dedicated to my friend, colleague, and mentor, the late Lana L. Lenar—who led me to appreciate light, to design with light, and to harness and direct its power—and also to the colleagues, friends, and family members who have enlightened my journey.

CONTENTS

INTRODUCTION

In the beginning there was nothing. God said, "Let there be light!" And there was light. There was still nothing, but you could see a whole lot better.
  —Ellen DeGeneres

This is not a technical guide to lighting. Instead, it reflects what I've learned in my travels through time and experience, and it shares enough technical input to enable you to converse knowledgably with any electrician or contractor. Each chapter provides tips on how to design lighting for a specific room, be it a living room, kitchen, or laundry room. What you will read results from my career-long design work and is grounded in the years I also spent in theater—onstage, backstage, and in the wings. That experience reinforced my belief in the vast power of light and its infinite potential.

With new technology evolving before our eyes, we have come to realize that we can not only design with light and color but also use light like artists, as if we are painting. I am not a lighting designer, nor am I a lighting consultant. Rather, I am an interior designer who uses light to express and enhance my vision. I have simply gathered enough information to feel confident in how I use light, and I continue to learn and observe.

For me, lighting is a very specific and complex aspect of design. I am compelled to write about it mainly because of my perspective as an interior designer. Throughout my career, I have had to respond so often to questions about home lighting that I came to feel that the current state of lighting technology needed to be explored and explained. My goal for this book is to advance the concept of light as a primary resource in designing any home interior.

Although it has a beginning, middle, and end, this book is not meant to be absorbed sequentially. I hope, however, that it reads well enough to be enjoyed, cover to cover, chapter by chapter, on cold winter nights before a crackling fire. But I conceived it as a reliable reference work—a manual you can turn to for guidance on how to light any room in your home. I think it will be useful not only to designers and architects but also to developers, contractors, property managers, and landscapers—in short, to professionals involved in any aspect of home building and design, as well as lay readers eager to improve the quality of light in their homes.

I am confident that the content will be edifying to homeowners engaged in remodeling their existing homes or responding to lighting challenges in new-home designs. That's another reason I structured the book so that each chapter can stand alone. I wanted to ensure that you needn't feel compelled to read chapter 4, for example, if your primary interest falls within the scope of chapter 7 or 8. Also, I have tried to contain the content in a handy package that is readily accessible, whether on a desk or bookshelf or in a valise or backpack to be carried when shopping for lighting products.

Today's so-called lighting revolution, which began soon after the turn of the twenty-first century, follows more than a hundred years of stasis: incandescent lighting that ultimately blanketed the world as a result of Thomas Alva Edison's late-nineteenth-century breakthrough invention. Since then, the incandescent lightbulb has assumed many forms and been shaped and sized for a variety of fixtures. Other types of residential lighting, all of which I will pinpoint and explain in the chapters ahead, gradually began to require other home-lighting sources.

Although none has had the impact of the latest LEDs, all have been leaders in furthering the lighting revolution.

These changes have become ongoing challenges. So whenever I have a project that I feel requires particularly thoughtful illumination, I will engage a professional lighting designer or lighting consultant who can bring a more knowledgeable and creative perspective to the project. It is not simply a matter of knowing what I want to light but what fixtures, lamps, and lightbulbs to specify, to maximize an effective and creative interior-lighting solution.

I can say for certain that specifying fixtures is a complex process, one that often becomes as confusing as controlling the flow of light itself. That's why I often turned to my lighting designer, the late Lana Lenar, of zeroLux Lighting Design, to assist me in crafting an in-depth lighting plan. Much of my knowledge of residential lighting has come from working with her.

My overall understanding of light has come mainly from my affiliation with the Designers Lighting Forum (DLF) of New York. I have served on its board of directors for decades, attending the monthly programs that have shared information I could not have obtained elsewhere. The organization's annual LEDucation is a two-day symposium, hosted by the DLF in New York City, that defines and explores advances in all aspects of LED lighting. It's an event that can seem overwhelming to a novice, but extracting core information from the experience is certain to make you feel more adept at using light fully and appropriately in home design. My membership has proved to be an invaluable exposure to advancements in lighting technology and usage.

Progress is swift and unending in the world of home lighting. There will always be new products, new concepts, and new procedures to recognize and engage.

But by using this book as a reference tool, you can feel confidently up to date about the information I share, because I have included scan tags, or QR codes, to link you to the latest developments and sources of product information from the lighting industry's major players. Because I have come to feel that one of the best ways to understand much of the intricacy of lighting design is through knowledge of available product, my scan tags will appear throughout this book to connect you to the websites of major lighting providers. Simply pushing a button will lead you to the leading providers and the latest sources of new products.

Understanding the science and application of light can be a lifelong learning commitment. The more we ask, the more we will know and the better our designs will be—and most important, the more we can see these designs in relation to the purpose for which they were imagined and developed. So, as you read this book, keep in mind that I have written it not only to share information and insight but also to inspire you to ask new and even more challenging questions.

—Charles Pavarini III

Ideas at one time were simple, like incandescent bulbs.

Beyond the tall oval doorway is a transitional living room subtly lit by LEDs embedded in the plaster ceiling. Additional room lighting is supplied by LEDs concealed behind the crown molding. Design by Pavarini Design, Inc.
Photograph: © Marco Ricca Studio

A Light Look Ahead

For people who currently have to burn fossil fuels to produce meager, polluting light, LED lighting is a game changer.
— Shuji Nakamura, cowinner of the 2014 Nobel Prize for Physics

"Light is a powerful thing," says Theo Richardson, director of development at the Brooklyn, New York–based firm Rich Brilliant Willing, known for its striking designs of LED fixtures. Richardson, who founded the firm in 2007 with partners Charles Brill and Alexander Williams, believes that "the right light lifts the mood, motivates us, and inspires productivity. At home, light enlivens the little things—our morning routines, the moments we spend with friends."

The future is always challenging, and never more so than now, particularly in the world of residential lighting. Consider this: until recently, very little had happened to alter the form or function of standard light sources since Thomas Alva Edison perfected the long-burning incandescent bulb, with the small addition of low-voltage halogen—a sister to incandescent. That was in 1879, more than a century ago. Think of the vast world of change that's taken place since then—in the way we live and the huge array of conveniences that have improved our lives.

Science and technology have joined forces to make life at home easier, more efficient, and more comfortable. There are new ways to heat, cool, and control our homes and protect them from the elements; new ways to store and cook food so meals can be made faster and more efficiently; new ways to capture sunlight and bring the outdoors virtually inside our living spaces.

In the world of residential lighting, change is also underway. Most incandescent lighting has been phased out and will essentially vanish, except to supply special needs. The result is that most of us have had to change the way we regard and utilize our electric-light sources. This has been particularly challenging because we were accustomed to what we call "natural light," which has traditionally been incandescent.

This is not the first time we have had to adjust for color temperature. Before electricity, our sources of artificial light were limited to fire and candlelight. As you're probably aware, a flame is much more orange than sunlight and has a significantly different quality. There's no doubt, however, that consumers enthusiastically embraced the transition from candlelight to incandescent light—available at the flip of a switch—despite its color differences.

Can you imagine anyone saying, "I don't know if Edison's new lightbulb is a good idea—it's not like what I'm used to in my gas lanterns." The Edison bulb delivered a very close approximation of natural sunlight, not candlelight. People adjusted, just as we're having to now. Meanwhile, new ways are being sought to mimic the sun's glow as incandescent lighting slowly vanishes from retailers' shelves.

Frankly, I don't think we can ever totally emulate the glow of the incandescent bulb, but I'm confident we'll be able to get close to it, and I think the focus should *not* be to match incandescent light but to try to match the tone of sunlight. My choice would be to abandon our thoughts and concerns about incandescents completely—in other words, move forward and not look back.

New Lighting Possibilities

The era of LEDs is upon us. These three initials stand for light-emitting diodes. It's hardly a futuristic concept—LEDs have been widely used in commercial situations for years, and the interior and exterior lights on most late-model cars are LEDs, each more powerful for their size than comparable incandescent, low-voltage, or HID (high-intensity discharge) lighting. LEDs were an accidental discovery that occurred in 1961 during a course of experiments conducted by two engineers, James R. Biard and Gary Pittman, at Texas Instruments.

A year later, a scientist at General Electric named Nick Holonyak Jr. developed the first commercially practical LED. It became known as a "visible-spectrum LED," because the color red it emitted was visible to the human eye, unlike those invisible infrared beams we're familiar with on TV remote controls. Holonyak's efforts earned him recognition as "father of the light-emitting diode." In 1963, he boldly predicted that LEDs would one day replace incandescent lightbulbs. He was certainly prescient; in the decades since then, LEDs have evolved to embrace a growing number of applications for home use. Different-colored LEDs can be used in electronics for digital displays, and when combined in great multiples (known as an array), they can even be arranged to become HD TV screens.

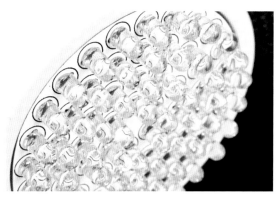

Multiple diodes, which pros call an array of LEDs, are needed to achieve the light output of a single LED bulb.

On average, the rated life of the old 100-watt incandescent bulb—the lighting industry calls it a *lamp*—is about 1,000 hours. By contrast, most LED bulbs/lamps are expected to last some 20,000 to 50,000 hours, which translates into ten or twenty years of regular use and suggests little likelihood of bulb replacements during a project lifetime.

LEDs' comparative wattage is low; they consume a minimal amount of energy and emit comparatively little heat. *Wattage* refers to the amount of energy an incandescent bulb consumes; our newest lighting sources are rated in *lumens*, the measurement of brightness. For example, an LED bulb whose light output is equal to that of a 60-watt incandescent bulb measures 800 lumens, as shown in this chart.

EFFICIENCY	Least			Most
BULB TYPE				
LUMENS	STANDARD	HALOGEN	CFL	LED
450	40 W	29 W	9 W	8 W
800	60 W	43 W	14 W	13 W
1100	75 W	53 W	19 W	17 W
1600	100 W	72 W	23 W	20 W
RATED LIFE	1 year	1–3 years	6–10 years	15–25 years
SAVINGS	✕	up to 30%	up to 75%	up to 80%

This chart compares various lighting technologies, their lumen output, and their energy consumption.

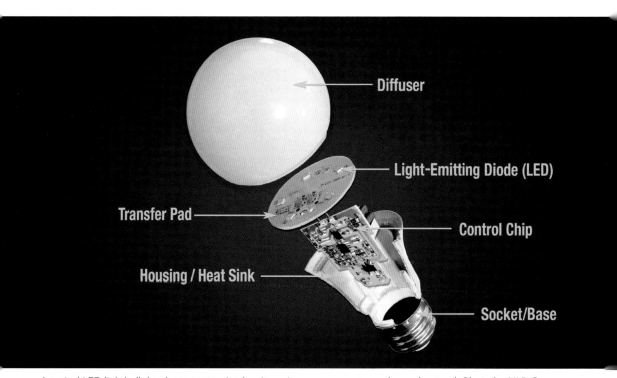

A typical LED lightbulb has been anatomized so its various components can be understood. *Photo by NLR-Green*

Most LED bulbs have their lumens value printed right on the bulb base. By contrast, most incandescent bulbs list their lumens value on the packaging. Look for the wattage rating and convert that to lumens, using the chart on page 125. Here are some guidelines:

• To replace a 100-watt incandescent bulb, look for an LED that emits about 1,500 lumens. If you prefer a softer look, opt for lower lumens; if you want brighter light, choose an LED with higher lumens.

• Replace a 75-watt bulb with an energy-saving LED yielding about 1,100 lumens.

• Replace a 60-watt bulb with an energy-saving LED that delivers about 800 lumens

• Replace a 40-watt bulb with an energy-saving LED that delivers about 450 lumens.

Calculating Lumens

To calculate how much artificial light a room will receive, simply add up the lumens of all the lightbulbs proposed for that space, and divide by the room's square footage to get the lumens per square foot. For a 120-square-foot room to be lit by a single overhead fixture housing two lightbulbs, each producing 800 lumens:

• 800 lumens + 800 lumens = 1,600 lumens

• 1,600 lumens to light 120 square feet = 13.3 lumens per square foot

A caveat: Although LEDs do not abruptly burn out like incandescent bulbs, their effectiveness is known to decrease slightly over time. Sometime after reaching the 50,000-hour mark, the light output will gradually drop to about 70 percent—lighting experts call this the L70 effect—which is the only way you would know that an LED bulb needs to be replaced.

Another caveat: The cost of LEDs was prohibitive for domestic use in the early years of their development—as high as $60 a bulb. But the price continues to shrink and at some point will likely be equal to incandescents. Some lighting experts predict that LEDs will continue dropping in price and energy use until the cost of lighting a home with white LEDs will sink to infinitesimal levels.

Of course, there are still some problems to solve. One involves *color temperature*, the actual color of light. It's measured in degrees kelvin (K). In many instances, the light issuing from LED bulbs is a very cool, almost ghostly white, whereas most of us have long been accustomed to the warm glow that incandescent bulbs emit—what we traditionally think of as light that closely emulates sunlight.

Other tones are certainly possible—some yellowish, some bluish. But it's unlikely that we'll ever enjoy exact matches to the incandescent bulb's quality and color.

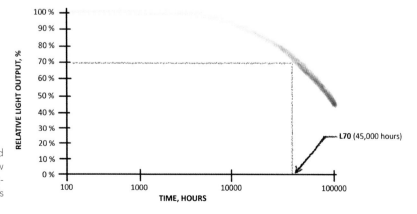

LUMEN DEPRECIATION FOR LEDs
L-70
ENERGY STAR SSL Criteria V.1.1 specifies minimum lifetime

* Lumen maintenace, L70: 25,000 hours for residential: 35,000 hours for commercial

L70 (45,000 hours)

RELATIVE LIGHT OUTPUT, %

TIME, HOURS

The life span of an LED is tracked in a diagram that illustrates how the light output gradually diminishes after 70 percent of the LED's life span has passed.

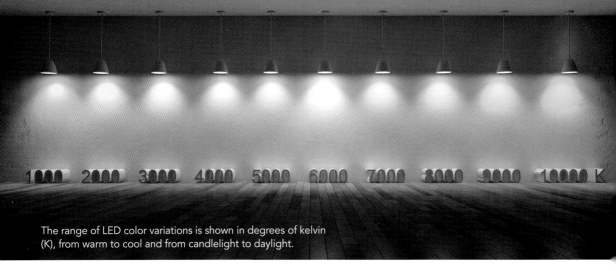

The range of LED color variations is shown in degrees of kelvin (K), from warm to cool and from candlelight to daylight.

1000   2000   3000   4000   5000   6000   7000   8000   9000   10000 K

As the global population continues to expand, more and more energy is destined to be consumed, squeezing our pocketbooks and taxing our planet's limited energy resources. LED lighting offers the advantage of very low energy consumption and very intense light. A number of lighting providers now market LEDs with lumens comparable to our most-used incandescents. These have become available in configurations that fit existing Edison bases as well as much-smaller candelabra bases, with no adapters required.

Although typical white LED lights appear to have no relation to the sun's warm glow, I feel confident that, over time, we will all learn to take advantage of their opportunities and efficiencies. Since LEDs have been lighting most commercial installations for some time—in large stores and offices—it's mainly our perception of home lighting that needs to change. Not so across much of Europe and Asia, where LED lighting has won wide acceptance and been used effectively for decades.

Colored LED bulbs comprise three nodes, each one no bigger than the tip of a ballpoint pen. These are called *RGB nodes* because each is a different color—red, green, or blue—but, combined in equal measure, they produce a type of white light.

Just as with paint color, literally millions of different hues stem from that trio of leading colors. Using a DMX controller, a device designed to tune the color of light, you can brighten or dim one or more of these nodes to achieve an infinite variety of tones. For a room setting at New York's Kips Bay Boys & Girls Club Decorator Show House, for example, I designed lighting that ranged from pale mauve to soft teal, transitions made possible by the use of computer-programmed LEDs.

Already achieving wide use are trinode LEDs, which combine red, green, and blue in a single node, instead of the cluster of separate RGB nodes we've been learning to work with. Color in each trinode is microscopically scaled, allowing designers to achieve various color effects. One problem is that manufacturers have little control over whether the resulting color is more blue, less blue, or even purple. However, new LED technology has given us RGB-A (the "A" stands for amber), thus creating a color option that comes much closer to mimicking sunlight. Indeed, in an attempt to truly mimic daylight, some RGB nodes add this fourth—amber, yellow, or white—to produce a better "white" light.

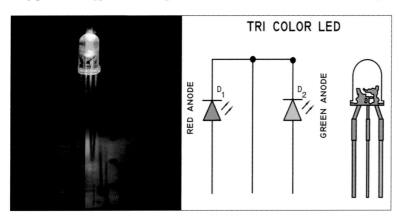

Beside an image of a trinode LED, with its red, green, and blue factors, a diagram illustrates how these RGBs can be blended to produce desired lighting colors.

The LED Advantage

LEDs yield a variety of tones, the result of manufacturers adding to the components of each bulb. Red, green, and blue can be achieved easily from RGB bulbs, but, until recently, white has been a major challenge. Since LED white continues to be cooler than incandescent white, manufacturers are intensely focused on improving the white color range of their LED products, striving to achieve lighting that's closer in tone to the familiar and comforting hue of sunlight. Some manufacturers have already devised a way to coat the glass surrounding their lamping with a yellow phosphor coating, which turns a slightly bluish tint into recognizable warm white.

LED bulbs are becoming more versatile and efficient. With some bulbs as small as tiny buttons, LEDs are more adaptable than incandescents to specific lighting tasks. For example, installed in a cove near the ceiling, they act like buried footlights to illuminate the periphery of a room.

Because they generate comparatively little heat, LED strip lights can be placed safely near upholstery and integrated *within* pieces of furniture. And they can be mounted on thin strands of tape for use as strip lighting. The smaller this tape or strip gets, the smaller the nodes are within them. Also, the less heat they emit, the more flexible the lighting becomes. Placing them in proximity to fabric is something I could never have done with incandescents.

Through OLEDs (organic light-emitting diodes), fabric can even become its own light source. How? An organic LED is a solid-state semiconductor, the result of placing two or three layers of organic film (each about 200 times thinner than a single human hair, if you can imagine it) between two conductors and applying electrical current. The result is a flexible, durable, super-lightweight source of bright light.

A halo of LEDs outlining this headboard is one example of how manipulating the RGB within a fixture can achieve different lighting effects. Their minimal heat output allows LEDs to be used near textiles. *Photo by Doug Holt Photography*

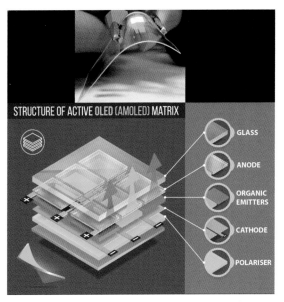

In the top photo, OLED light is infused into a clear substrate. The diagram shows the structure of an OLED and the materials it's made of.

Manufacturers have found ways to infuse OLED lighting directly into paper-thin sheets of polymer plastic, a lightweight organic material used in displays for cellphones and TV sets. It's also likely to find its way into residential use in the form of ambient lighting. Thus the lightbulb of the future may not be a lightbulb at all. Instead of dealing with a filament that illuminates when electrified, we may find ourselves choosing a type of fabric that illuminates when energized.

This swatch of lighted wallpaper shows how tiny LEDs can be incorporated into a variety of decorative products. *Courtesy of Mestyle LED Wallpaper*

What about illuminated wall coverings? This, too, is an innovative concept. Some aspects of a wall-covering pattern, rather than the entire wall, could be lit and dimmed as desired to add delicate hints of light to your walls. The possibilities seem endless—using light in new ways and in places where it never existed before.

Think about it: Even your carpeting can be illuminated, as long as there's a link to a power source. And what about upholstery and curtain fabrics? Integrating OLED lighting into textiles and wall coverings could create a truly magical experience that wouldn't compromise the material's beauty, texture, softness, or durability.

LEDs mounted on tape and connected to a power source can be tucked behind molding to accent architecture. Or you can place it behind a piece of furniture or under a cabinet to achieve a subtle focus. Lighting a room creatively with LEDs can be a way to draw the eye to a particular area or object. With LEDs, you can create a light source that's any size, shape, or configuration. A thin wire from the LED tape would connect to a hidden LED driver box.

All of us will need to change the way we think about using color and light in our rooms and about how the new source of light affects our perception of interior colors. Long experience has taught me that even plain walls look different under different light sources. Everyone will be challenged as the use of incandescent lighting fades.

Other Home Lighting Alternatives

I believe we are more tolerant of the lighting in commercial spaces than in our homes. When we visit an office building or a mall, we're there for a comparatively short span of time and accept the lighting for what it is. But when we bring it into our homes, we're more demanding and critical. I often hear people say, "I just want my rooms to have good light."

That is the challenge—to choose the type of light that best befits how we want to experience our home interiors. LEDs are not the only choice. Some lightbulb manufacturers have been producing improved and more-energy-conscious incandescents. And other choices have existed for some time:

Compact fluorescents (CFLs) typically fit the Edison sockets that incandescents screw into, but their life is more than eight times longer. CFLs are rarely marketed now because the inside of each sealed bulb, or tube, contains a mercury coating. That has made their disposal challenging. If the glass breaks, toxic mercury will be released. No surprise, then, that CFLs have been supplanted by LEDs.

Coiled for optimum light output, a typical compact fluorescent lightbulb (CFL) is shaped to achieve maximum light output.

Halogen lighting is basically an incandescent bulb with a tungsten filament. Sealed within that bulb is an inert gas plus a trace amount of halogen (iodine or bromine). Conceived back in 1882 but not considered commercially viable for another half century, halogens began being developed commercially in the 1950s. It was then that two scientists at General Electric, Elmer Fridrich and Emmet Wiley, focused on halogen use as a potentially economical way of projecting 8-millimeter film. Since then, of course, halogens' popularity has expanded. Smaller than incandescents, they consume less energy and can last more than twice as long and at higher color temperatures.

TUNGSTEN-HALOGEN LAMPS

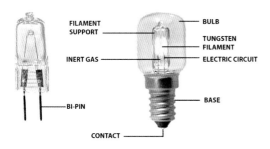

In these halogen bulb diagrams, one shows a socket that screws in, the other a bipin plug-in bulb.

A low-voltage MR16 halogen bulb is dimmable and more closely color-true than a comparable LED, and its configuration is unique. It bounces light to the back of the bulb, which is cone shaped and faceted, then projects the light forward and out. For residential designers, variable beam spread is another one of halogen's main assets. When an incandescent light is switched on, its beam radiates in all directions. You can dim it, of course, but to shape or control the beam spread you would need special light fixtures. With halogens, beam spread is a function of the bulb itself. Your choice of bulb determines the beam width, depending on what you want to illuminate.

Here are typical MR-16 halogen reflector bulbs with bipin bases, typically used in recessed lighting and track lighting fixtures.

Halogens are used to light displays in retail stores and boutiques. Their light quality gives a sparkle to whatever is being lit—diamonds in a high-end jewelry store window, for example. In home design, halogens are unrivaled in their ability to focus a narrow beam of light on key objects. A pin spot will make a piece of sculpture visually pop, looking bright and literally washed in light. Halogens are also favored for use in desk and reading lamps and outdoor lighting systems.

An LED MR-16 bulb is shown with various diffusers that can be used to affect a light's beam spread.

Halogens became popular because they were so much smaller than incandescent lamps. The filament inside an incandescent lightbulb can be only so small, because human hands or sometimes a special machine must be employed to insert it. Before halogens, powerful parabolic aluminized reflector lamps (PARs) were used as high-output recessed lights, locomotive headlights, and aircraft landing lights. Today, a tiny halogen is capable of yielding what each of these giant light sources could deliver. Think of the early computers. When first introduced, a single computer filled an entire room; now you can hold one in your hand and even stash it in a pocket.

Another benefit is that halogens come in a wide variety of shapes and sizes. By contrast, incandescent bulbs always retain the same basic parameters; their glass enclosures, or envelopes, cannot be molded or shaped in any special way. In essence, what you see is what you get. Halogens have drawbacks, however. They get much hotter than regular incandescent bulbs—their high temperatures are essential to their function and must be handled carefully with a paper towel or gloves. **You can even get a sunburn with long-term exposure** to the ultraviolet (UV) rays from uncoated or unfiltered halogens. They are also easily damaged by surface contamination, so if you touch a hot halogen bulb, the natural oil on your fingertips could concentrate the heat and cause the bulb to explode. To prevent damage or injury, a grid, glass lens, or grille is often used to protect the bulb in case it explodes. Unlike CFLs, though, halogens contain no mercury and can be disposed of easily. The MR 16 halogen's one requirement is a transformer to change the 120-volt power to 12 volt.

Xenon lighting was developed in 1940s Germany to replace the cumbersome carbon-arc lamps that were used to project films in movie theaters. Marketed as high-intensity discharge lamps, xenons have no filaments. Each bulb lights up when an arc between two tungsten-metal electrodes is created within it. A xenon bulb yields five times more light than its halogen equivalent and can last up to ten times longer. Because its light is a cooler color than an incandescent bulb but warmer than a comparable halogen, it's been a popular choice for designers of greenhouses and indoor gardens. A xenon bulb's color temperature is often described as being close to that of the noonday sun—in a clear sky, of course.

Xenons have also found their way inside the home, most commonly as under-cabinet lighting. They are widely used on bookcases, cabinet interiors, wall-hung artwork, staircases, and reading lamps and in garages. In addition, these bulbs have displaced halogens in the design of some automobile headlights. The long life and low energy consumption of xenon bulbs effectively offset their relatively high initial cost. One significant caveat: They cannot be used to illuminate oil or acrylic paintings. Exposure to xenon light will literally destroy the pigment.

Cold cathode lights evolved in Great Britain soon after the Edison lamp received its United States patent. Technically defined as a transducer, which converts electrical energy into light energy, cold cathode lights are close cousins of both CFLs and neon lamps. Though they differ somewhat from their relatives, they are the preferred choice to light neon signs in places where temperatures drop well below freezing. They're also a good choice for difficult-to-access locations where long-life light sources are required—they last 45,000 to 60,000 hours (London's landmark Big Ben timepiece is a prime example). Occasionally, cold cathode lighting has also been specified in home settings instead of CFLs because they are dimmable and their light is easier on the eyes.

Fiber optics, used mostly in telecommunication and computer networking, are bundles of flexible, transparent fibers—either silica glass or plastic. Only slightly thicker than a human hair, each fiber can transmit up to a hundred different "messages," far more than a traditional copper cable. Manipulating light by refraction was first demonstrated in the 1840s by two French

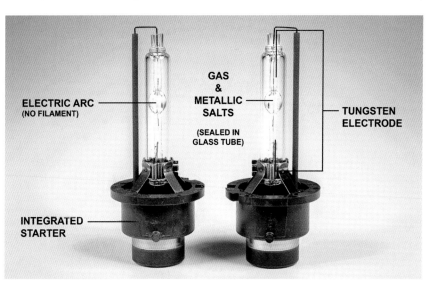

Components of a xenon lamp: note there is no filament; an electric arc supplies the light.

scientists, Daniel Colladon and Jacques Babinet. Eighty years later, fiber-optic applications were finding their way into medical and dental examination rooms all over the world. And by the 1930s, these bundled fibers were receiving a transparent coating that made image transmission even more efficient. Fiber optics are widely used in home security systems, which are programmed to respond to any intrusion with a resounding alarm.

Consider the Future

In the years ahead, I think we will see a greater-than-ever mix of lighting methods as designers and specifiers become increasingly creative in using and manipulating various sources of light. I can't imagine any designer, now or in the future, saying, "Okay, I'm going to use only xenon or LED lighting." I look to the coordinated use of LEDs, halogens, xenons, and other more specialized forms of lighting in designing home interiors.

What's prompting all these changes? The answer is development of new technology, spurred, of course, by our need to slash energy consumption. EDs are at the forefront of this twenty-first-century lighting revolution, and not only because of their stingy energy use but because they are mercury free, unlike fluorescents and compact fluorescents. In fact, no discussion of sustainable green design can even begin without LEDs entering the conversation. Concern about sustainability is securely locked into our collective consciousness. In the years ahead, green design will become even more important in the way we shape and inhabit our homes as new conservation methods, materials, and techniques continue to emerge and be refined.

At present, I, more than my clients, am advocating the use of these new developments. In contrast, Europeans have generally been savvier about energy consumption, and thus more receptive to change. In recent years, I have stayed at many a European hotel where my key card must be slipped into a slot to activate the room lights. Leaving the room, I remove the key card from its slot and have only a few seconds to exit before the lights go out. While some people may find it annoying, it's really just a small gesture that over time can save significant energy.

Wrinkles and Reservations

Currently there is no regulation governing chromatics—the way colors appear under various lighting conditions. The result is that the color appearance of LED bulbs rated 3000K varies considerably among manufacturers. They are not required to make sure their products maintain exactly 3000K, even if that's how these items are marketed. In fact, a 10 percent range is considered okay. So it falls to the consumer or designer to test for the accuracy of lightbulbs' color temperature.

I recall, in particular, a vintage chandelier that my design team and I obtained for a Park Avenue apartment. The fixture was 12 feet tall and was installed directly above a 22-foot-high winding staircase. I chose to light this chandelier with LEDs mainly because of their long life. I knew there would be no easy way to reach the light fixture once the scaffolding was gone.

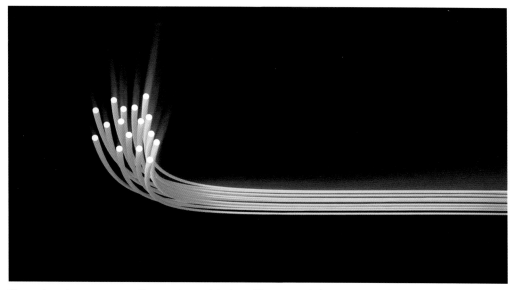

Shown here is a transparent fiber-optic conduit that will transport light to a remote location.
Image courtesy of LEDLighting-HUT.com

A 12-foot-tall Venini chandelier lit entirely by LEDs is suspended some 20 feet above the ground floor of a New York City penthouse. Design by Pavarini Design, Inc. *Photograph: © Marco Ricca Studio*

So I went online and selected 3000K bulbs that were described as being compatible with one another. We had to do a lot of mockups because some of the bulbs had diodes that were directed out from the lamp, while others had diodes directed sideways. After installing the bulbs and switching on the fixture, I found that a few slight differences persisted (one bulb seemed too blue and altered the colors being lit).

Are such differences evident to the average consumer? Well, if you made a very detailed comparison, yes, but they would be perceived more as a difference in contrast than in color. Let's say you were looking at different lights through rose-tinted glasses; everything would be uniformly colored, so only the contrast would be discernible.

Think of the flame from a match. Better yet, think of a multicolored blowtorch flame that's hot enough to melt metal. In either case, the flame will appear really blue in the center, where the heat is highly condensed. Along the periphery is where you'll see, first, the red, then the orange and yellow—the yellow getting paler as it moves toward white—and, finally, blue. Contrast is minimal when looking at sky blue, rated at 10000K, but as you move down the kelvin scale, you'll see that the contrast increases. Thus, if you're looking at red (candlelight: 1000K) or orange (early sunrise: 2000K), the contrast will be pretty obvious.

Progress Is Unending

Sometime in the future, we may no longer need to use actual light fixtures, except perhaps decoratively. Imagine entering a beautifully lit room with no visible light source. Maybe our architecture will actually light our rooms—fixture-free illumination that's also wireless as well as remotely controlled (if it wasn't wireless, we would have to break into each interior wall and install wiring).

Dimming systems now exist that are entirely remote. A single "brain" can be installed in a closet, with modules placed on walls in various parts of a home. What "remote" means is that the power supply and the driver (the direct link to your light source) can be located away from both the source of light and the source of power. The driver is like a computer code that tells your light source how bright or dim the light should be.

I could install such a system simply by replacing the switch with a control module that would "speak" to that brain installed discreetly in one of my closets. Each control zone or switch leg would have one of these modules, so they would *all* speak to the brain. To activate the brain, I would need to acquire a control pad small enough to be carried, so I could regulate all the lighting from wherever I happened to be in my home.

That control could, of course, be a smartphone, tablet, or any mobile computer controlled by a remotely located device. Another possibility could be pretty cool: What if, instead of lampshades filtering the light from lightbulbs, the lampshades themselves lit up? I know of a company that has been developing a type of tape that could be integrated into lampshade fabric, so that in effect, the lampshade could become a light source, eliminating the bulb. Table lamps are decorative and can be attractive, but someday they may be needed only to support light-bearing lampshades.

Here's yet another option that isn't as fanciful as it may seem: imagine a glass-topped coffee table as a light source. When you run your hand over or under the glass, the heat from your hand would make the tabletop light up. Also note that remote-controlled, battery-operated LED lights can be installed on walls or ceilings, in closets, in or over cabinets—all without wiring. You could manipulate your home's lighting just by pushing a few buttons on a mobile device.

A typical driver, the brains of an LED, will function remotely to control each aspect of lighting output, including brightness and color. *Photo courtesy of JESCO Lighting*

SCAN

CODE

JESCO

Illumination is elusive. You can't touch it; you can't feel it, except for the heat it may generate. A good designer will make sure no one is aware of the lighting's technical aspects. The idea is to enable people to *experience* light—see its effects without being aware of the power source. So, whether it's recessed lighting, cove lighting, or a spotlight pinpointing a decorative object, a gifted designer will never emphasize where the light is coming from, only what is illuminated. You, the viewer, should be concerned only with how you're affected by light.

Decades from now, perhaps it will be possible to harness phosphorescence. Its effect would be like what you'd experience walking on a beach in Hawaii—specifically on the north shore of the island of Kauai—where at night the phosphorescent sand illuminates every step you take. Now *that* would be some experience to bring home. The potential is limitless.

Achieving Quality of Light in Any Room

Lumen Recommendations

The following guidelines relate to general room lighting, such as that provided by standard ceiling fixtures or multiple lamps. In areas intended for work or reading, you'd likely include additional focused light (task lighting) to brighten locations where light is crucial—kitchen countertops, for example.

Lighting experts recommend the following light levels for key rooms in a home:

- living room: 10 to 20 lumens per square foot
- dining room: 30 to 40 lumens per square foot
- bedroom: 10 to 20 lumens per square foot
- bathroom: 70 to 80 lumens per square foot
- hallways: 5 to 10 lumens per square foot
- kitchen (general lighting): 30 to 40 lumens per square foot
- kitchen (task areas): 70 to 80 lumens per square foot
- laundry room: 70 to 80 lumens per square foot

These guidelines relate to overall room lighting, such as what standard ceiling fixtures or multiple lamps would provide. In areas intended for reading or working, you would likely include additional focused light (task lighting) to brighten specific locations where light is crucial, such as a kitchen's work zone or countertop area.

A Hawaiian beach sparkles with bioluminescent particles. *Photo © Doug Perrine*

Topping an antique lamp, this custom shade is adorned with brush fringe, silk-covered uprights, and an opened gallery. Design by Pavarini Design, Inc. *Photograph: Doug Holt Photography*

Lampshade Lore

Light is the first element of design; without it there is no color, form, or texture.
—Thomas E. Farin, educator, lighting consultant, entrepreneur

Lighting is central to successful room design. It creates focus in ways that no other design discipline can, inviting us to experience an interior in a unique way. Many room-design challenges can be met by the choice of lampshades. Used appropriately, they provide a valuable opportunity to add to a room's decorating story. Never underestimate how the shape, size, color, and pattern of a lampshade can expand its influence and power. In the choice of lampshades and diffusers, we can make lighting an integral part of almost any room design.

Lampshades were originally created to reduce the glare of flame-produced torches and candlelight, which had a very reddish or red-orange tone that could be hard on the eye. The flames later produced by gas and then oil were softer and whiter in tone. But even the brightest lamps provided less light than a modern 25-watt incandescent bulb.

The first known lampshades were strictly utilitarian, their purpose not just to soften and disperse light. It was in seventeenth-century Paris that lampshades came into wide use—mostly in the light standards that lined city streets. Standing tall to illuminate the night, these oil-burning fixtures distributed light through their glass shades. Inside, a dome-shaped gas reflector at the top of each fixture would direct the light beams downward, toward the street. Another reflector below the light source—this one slightly concave—would shoot light outward. The amount of output from these light standards was impressive. No wonder Paris became known as La Vie Lumière, the City of Light.

In the early 1800s, German-born inventor Frederick Albert Winsor achieved a breakthrough. For the first time, gas produced in his London factory was distributed through a vast pipeline to city streets and then to homes. Gas light was efficient but its fumes were deadly without ventilation, and there was a risk of combustion. Later, oil became the more efficient and effective fuel choice. Several wicks were used inside each light standard to extend the illumination. I imagine they were made of whatever fabric was found to burn readily. With the Edison invention, the filaments sealed inside electric bulbs were fashioned from vegetable fiber, but eventually, bamboo was popular because it burned slowly. A shift to longer-burning metal-alloy filaments was followed by a preference for tungsten in the early years of the twentieth century. That's when artificial light became really harsh and shades became mandatory—and, ultimately, fashionable.

A lantern streetlamp directed light down to the street in 1860s Paris.

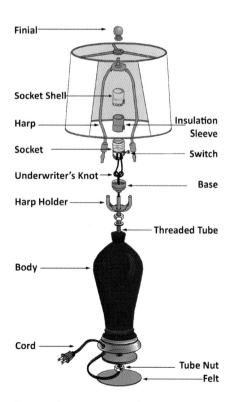

Finial
Socket Shell
Harp
Socket
Underwriter's Knot
Harp Holder
Body
Cord
Insulation Sleeve
Switch
Base
Threaded Tube
Tube Nut
Felt

These are the components of a typical table lamp.

Shades in Decoration

Shortly after Edison's breakthrough, lampshades were recognized for their great decorative potential, as intrinsic to design as the fixtures themselves. In the Victorian era, odd-shaped lampshades became highly fashionable, some with fringe or beading at the bottom, others pleated and decorated with colorful rosettes.

That was a time when everything decorative was ornamented in some way, from the arm of a chair to the base of a sofa and the top and bottom of a lampshade. Soon lampshades began showing up in odd shapes, with fabrics stretched over shaped armatures. In wide use then was something like nylon, except that nylon hadn't been invented yet. Loosely woven, this fabric's warp and weft were easily manipulated, so it could be stretched to accommodate some of that era's truly unusual lampshade creations.

Over-the-top opulence: that is the only way to describe what America's Louis Comfort Tiffany achieved in his late-nineteenth-century lampshade designs. One of his breakthrough efforts involved shades made of stained-glass mosaics in exuberant patterns.

His signature design was the Dragonfly lampshade, whose tiny pieces of colored glass were held in place by a soldering procedure, as in stained-glass window making (an original Dragonfly shade is probably worth tens of thousands of dollars today). Such shades were produced in multiples on an assembly line. Today, these same designs are being reproduced in various forms in a whole range of materials. But light travels best through glass; plastic and other materials absorb some of the emitted light.

Stemming from Tiffany's trendsetting efforts were reverse painted designs—glass shades with an artist's pattern painted on the inside.

To achieve this effect, a design was traced onto a glass shade's inner surface and then colorfully painted by an artisan. When the light is off, the design looks milky and faint because of the thickness of the glass, but when the light is switched on, the whole pattern is visible and the shade comes alive. This technique led to embossed glass shades, in which decorative elements, such as fruit or flowers, were rendered in relief and then reverse-painted.

As the twentieth century began, other materials became part of the lampshade vocabulary: plastics and celluloid, for example. Then, in the art deco era of the 1920s and '30s, a totally new form of plastic, Bakelite, began receiving strong interest. Also, by then, designers and craftsmen were experimenting with cut glass, looking critically at what happens when light is filtered through colored-glass fragments. Some of them were polished to enhance the effectiveness of light passing directly through the glass. Other pieces were sandblasted, diffusing the light and softening the glare.

I've seen a great many art deco fixtures with geometric patterns cut into the glass, thus projecting light in decorative ways onto a ceiling or floor. A lampshade's function is not only to reduce glare but also to disperse light in a particular way.

Louis Comfort Tiffany's original bronze-patinated Dragonfly bronze table lamp design called for a stained-glass shade.

Designed to soften a lamp's glare, this decorative hurricane shade was made of embossed and sand-blasted glass. *Photo courtesy of B&P Lamp Supply*

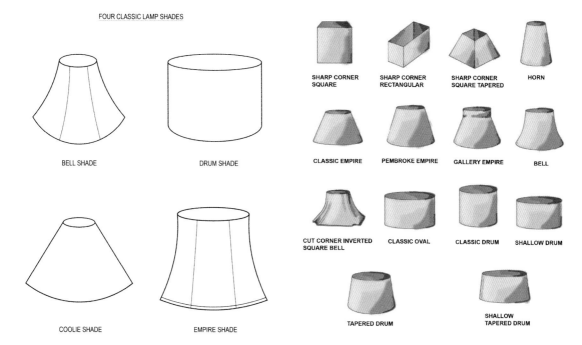

FOUR CLASSIC LAMP SHADES

BELL SHADE

DRUM SHADE

COOLIE SHADE

EMPIRE SHADE

SHARP CORNER SQUARE

SHARP CORNER RECTANGULAR

SHARP CORNER SQUARE TAPERED

HORN

CLASSIC EMPIRE

PEMBROKE EMPIRE

GALLERY EMPIRE

BELL

CUT CORNER INVERTED SQUARE BELL

CLASSIC OVAL

CLASSIC DRUM

SHALLOW DRUM

TAPERED DRUM

SHALLOW TAPERED DRUM

These are examples of other lampshade configurations.

Shape and Structure

Take a look at lampshades online, in a showroom, or in a retail store. You'll see that they are rendered in four basic shapes, each with its own set of variations and each critical to the way you present the light source.

• the inward-curving bell shape and the classic drum shape, which is strictly straight sided.

• the so-called coolie shape, narrow at the top, with a severe slope toward a wide bottom

• The regency or empire shape, in which the shade's top opening is precisely half that of the bottom, creating a standard slope, no matter how big or small the shade

The empire has become the go-to style because it can be rendered in many diverse ways. The fabric might be shirred or pleated, and if the latter, the pleats could be vertical, diagonal, or swirled around the entire surface of the shade, from top to bottom. Variations are possible, of course. Not all shades are round. Some standard examples are oval, square, rectangular, and octagonal.

Today we're seeing anamorphic lampshades—with unconventional shapes, like clouds. Particularly with ceiling fixtures, either surface-mounts or chandeliers, it's possible to see a vast variety of anamorphic shades in a single showroom.

Lampshades are made from a variety of materials, although silk remains the most luminous. Some high-end designs are shaped from hides, which are particularly popular in Colorado and the American Southwest.

Shades crafted from this natural material are translucent, unlike silk. A natural hide emits an amber glow, almost like mica. This material must be oiled annually to prevent drying out and cracking.

Mica, a type of stone, was used widely in the arts-and-crafts movement of the late nineteenth century. It's a hardy natural material that can be sliced thinly without compromising its stability. As a result, wires or uprights are not needed for support. When sliced, it's translucent. When lit, it has an amber or silver tone. Depending on the shape you choose, a mica shade can direct light up or down.

Horsehair is another material choice. I have used it often, notably in the living room of a Kips Bay Decorator Show House, where one of our table lamps had a blue-dyed horsehair shade. The look was distinctive; it had texture, and, like no other material, horsehair can be bent or twisted. And because it's natural hair, it doesn't ever crease. After it has been bleached, it can be dyed any color. I've even had it produced in orange to create a unique look in a living-room setting.

Horsehair is not stable enough to hold a shape, however, so it needs a frame. Its diaphanous quality approaches that of cellophane. Hold it up to a sunlit window, and you'll see that it's surprisingly translucent because of the way it's woven. I've even used it for window shades. Horsehair is sold by the yard as a textile and available only in 26-inch widths, due to the usual length of a horse's tail!

With any type of shade fabric, you will need a wire armature on which to sew the material. Depending on the spread of the frame, it will require at least four vertical supports. The result is that when the light is on, that structural rib is not apparent. An alternative is an upright design with vertical ribs that stand slightly back from the face of the shade, as though leaning toward the light source. This type of discreet armature would not be visible. Nowadays it's possible to find ready-mades that come with this clever setback, and if you opt for paper instead of fabric, note that except for rings at the top and bottom, you won't need an armature at all. The paper will hold the shape of the shade.

Beyond the standard forms, you can find distinctive handmade shades at custom establishments. Here in New York City, the Ruth Vitow company was run by two sisters with bright-red hair who bickered continually while turning out shades that were truly extraordinary. I remember their factory as a step back in time, an Old World establishment whose workers, all women, sat around using needles and thread to attach hand-sewn fabric onto armatures.

The fabric wasn't simply sewed on; the whole armature was wrapped. One of the workers would make a ribbon out of a piece of the selected fabric and wind it tightly around each metal component—the uprights and horizontal sections—providing a convenient way for the shade cover to be sewn onto the frame. I know of only a few other crafts people who could produce hand-sewn lampshades that rivaled this company's work.

A variety of national lampshade retailers also do custom work when you have particular sizes and shapes in mind. As anyone restoring fine interiors will tell you, antique lamps may survive constant use and the passing of time, but the shades for vintage lamps rarely do. If

Designed by Abramczyk, woven off-white fabric wraps a cluster of white translucent textile cylinders clustered around multiple light sources, creating discs of light at the bottom of the shade. *Photograph: J. Randall Tarasuk*

Designer Ayala Serfaty's cloudlike flush-mount light fixtures bring an ethereal quality to this entry hall. Design by Drake/Anderson. *Photograph: © Marco Ricca Studio*

you can find the actual frame or a plausible likeness, however, a sensitive craftsman should be able to supply the covering—a material and style that re-creates the original or even achieves something different, if you want a look that's unique. There's no reason you can't change the material or even alter the shape. It's your choice.

How does a shade fit on a lamp? By means of a fitter, which is a type of wire that's usually crossed at the top, leaving an opening sized to fit over the stem that tops the harp. A washer goes on top of that stem, and a finial, which can be decorative or utilitarian, is screwed on to hold the shade firmly in place. There is also the Uno fitter, by which the lampshade's ring fits over the socket and is stabilized when a lightbulb is screwed in.

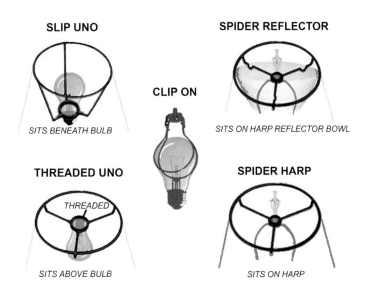

These five fitters illustrate how a shade can be connected to the body of a lamp.

Shade Size and Scale

The relationship between a lamp and its shade is one of design's imponderables. There's no formula other than this: a shade's height and width should be determined not only by the size of the lamp body but also by the height and width of its base.

Is the base tall and skinny or short and round? The only rule of thumb I can offer is that whatever shade you choose should hide from view the elements in the lamp's upright stem, or rod. These includes the lightbulb socket, the stem, and the on-and-off switch or dimmer at the top of the fixture or lamp.

In today's contemporary-style rooms, it's not unusual to place a small shade on a very tall lamp. My best advice is to take your lamp to a retail lighting store, place it on the counter, and try different-sized shades until your eye tells you the look is right.

My colleagues and I like putting shades on sconces that we treat like candles. If the "candle" is to be mounted close to a wall, consider using a shield instead of a conventional shade—a covering with a 180-degree curve. Leaving the back open will illuminate the wall behind the sconce.

The tall and short of it is illustrated in this pairing created to show how two different proportions can be paired to make a singular design statement. Design by Pavarini Design, Inc. *Photograph: Doug Holt Photography*

Options and Opportunities

Lampshades can be a design tool for reinforcing a particular style and ambience. They have the potential to become one of a room's major decorating features. That's because when you enter a room, your eye is naturally drawn to the light. You might also be attracted to the light fixtures, which usually express the feeling and style of a room, but the lampshades are among a room's main attractions.

Because a lampshade can be made out of any type of fabric, even burlap, what you choose depends on the room's decorating theme. If style dictates, the shade could be trimmed with fringe, beading, or embroidery. Why not consider some of the special fabrics and trims being imported from Europe? I've seen fabric that incorporates pieces of material sewn onto it in a loose way. And, yes, I've seen lamps covered in this kind of fabric; they make a very strong statement. My point is that a shade doesn't have to be ivory, or any particular color for that matter. You might find it interesting to use patterned or textured fabric to provide interest and detail.

Today you often see double shades—an opaque inner shade combined with an outer shade that sits an inch or so outside the inner shade and is usually made from a translucent fabric such as cheesecloth or sheer. The effect is that when you're looking into a lamp that's lit, you're seeing into the inner shade through its outer layer. The effect is one of very soft illumination, with the translucent material stylishly filtering the image.

Lampshades and LEDs

The use of LEDs has compelled us to shield or shade lights in ever more inventive ways. Increasingly, light is being supplied by minutely scaled LED fixtures in linear arrangements—sometimes also in circles, squares, or swirls—many them applied to strips of tape.

Whether installed in conventional straight lines or more inventively, LED tapes require some kind of diffuser or shield to spread projected light over an expanded area and also to ensure that the individual LED nodes are never visible. The word "diffuser," rather than "shade," is commonly used to describe this application. It refers to devices that also create a blurring effect, stretching out the beams of LED nodes to become a continuous ribbon of light.

The shield could be a shallow apron of metal or even wood. Due to their relatively low heat output, LEDs won't burn such surfaces. Choosing a soft-fabric diffuser would probably not be advisable, however; some kind of hard material, even plastic, would make the most

effective apron. Whatever material you choose, its design should not only shield those intensely bright LED nodes from view but also direct their light where desired.

Although the Edison bulb has remained essentially unchanged for about a hundred years, lampshades have continually evolved. Through their size, shape, pattern, and color, they play an important role in accentuating key interior spaces. As designers become bolder and more innovative, they are looking not only to the past for inspiration, but also to the future. As the concept of organic LEDs becomes more evolved, sources of illumination are destined to find their way, in minuscule forms, into fabrics, papers, and other thin materials. I look forward to the time when, with tiny organic LEDs embedded in the fabric—and, perhaps, with a simple wave of the hand—we will turn on our lampshades instead of our lamps.

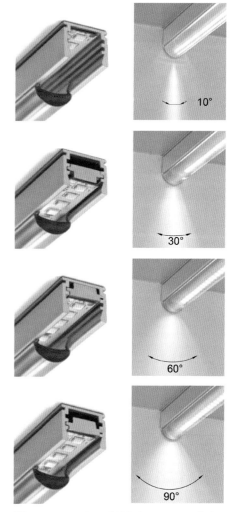

Four different examples of LED beam spread show how glare-reducers eliminate lighting hotspots.

Choosing a Lampshade

• Keep the room's design aesthetic in mind. Do you want the lamps and lampshades to be expressive or to blend in?

• Determine where your lamps and shades will be placed in the room. Where will they live in the space you've designed?

• What functions do your lamps need to fulfill, and how much light will these functions require?

• What is the light source each shade will be filtering? Will that light source generate glare that needs filtering?

• The shade should sit 2 or 3 inches away from the light source to avoid discoloration or the possibility of burning because of heat being generated, unless you are using LEDs.

• The style, size, and shape of your lamp base will help you decide whether the shade should be a decorative focus, or if the lamp itself is the main event.

Shade size guidelines for table lamps:

1. The height of a shade should be about three-quarters the height of the base.

2. The width of a shade should be roughly equal to the height of the lamp, from base to fitting.

3. To keep the lamp looking balanced, its shade should be at least ½ inch (⅓ cm) wider than the base on both sides.

4. A shade's shape should flatter and relate to the lamp form.

5. If you are having difficulty choosing between two sizes, it's usually better to choose the larger option (although small shades often suit very tall, thin lamps).

• Why not be daring and choose a print?

• Always trust your eye!

A chandelier utilizing OLED technology: suspension cables allow OLED discs in various lengths to hang from a ceiling-mounted canopy, creating the illusion of a chandelier. *Photo courtesy of Blackbody OLED*

The lighting is layered in a formal living room lit by table lamps, sconces, recessed lights, LED cove lighting, and a sofa-back table lit by RGB-LEDs. Design by Pavarini Design, Inc. Photograph: © Marco Ricca Studio

CHAPTER 3

In a Living-Room Mode

Design is defined by light and shade, and appropriate light is enormously important.
—Albert Hadley, interior designer

In interior design, light is a primary tool, not an afterthought: lighting ideas occur as I'm thinking about window treatments, furniture placement, architectural detailing, focal points, and the room's overall feel. It's hard for me to separate these elements; I see all of them in depth. Because of lighting's role in defining a style and creating a sense of well-being, it should be given the same importance as color, texture, and form.

By the time I begin designing a room, I've had multiple meetings with my clients to discuss how they'll use it. "How do you expect to live in the space?" I'll ask. "Are you going to use it mostly in the afternoon? In the evening? Do you entertain friends often, or will it be mostly occupied by family?" I'm especially eager to learn whether they want the room to be formal or casual, and how their lifestyle will be incorporated into that room. Do they plan to use it as kickback space for relaxing and resting their feet on an ottoman? Or do they see the space as being more curated, with beautiful furnishings, fabrics, and art?

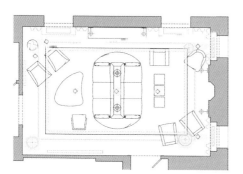

The answers will not only direct the design but also help me decide how to light it. And if the room is to be multifunctional, flexible lighting is at the heart of the plan. When developing a concept for any room, especially a living room, you must have a clear idea what you want the room to feel like. The lighting you choose will reinforce that idea.

In a lighting-concepts plan of the room at left, placement of direct, indirect, and decorative light sources is shown vis-à-vis the furniture floor plan.

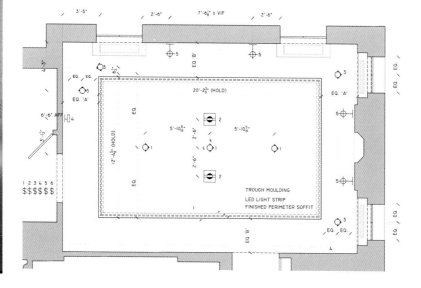

The reflected ceiling plan of the living room shown pinpoints the exact placement of all dimensions of installed lighting, plus electrical outlets for the custom illuminated sofa-back table.

Multipurpose Lighting

Living rooms have become much more versatile than they once were. Virtually gone are the days of living rooms that feel roped off visually, a place where you pause at the doorway and look in before being ushered into the kitchen or the family room, where your hosts assume you will feel more comfortable. The reality is that we no longer live in formal ways. There is a lot of crossover activity, not only in living rooms but in other rooms as well, which means that lighting should have the capacity to adjust to shifting needs

My firm was once asked to design a large living room for a client who wanted it to feel comfortable and accessible. Our solution was to install cabinetry for two desk areas and to bring in a sofa and chair that would invite a serious reader. We created a welcoming multiuse space, rather than a room reserved for special occasions. Many homes today do not have the luxury of rooms for separate uses. The living room really is a multipurpose space, and in these kinds of spaces we create adaptive lighting—illumination that's as appropriate for an evening of card playing or casual conversation as for staging a cocktail party. The arrangement and layering of light become extremely important. The lighting design must be balanced and embrace every potential function.

Today we have myriad lighting choices: ceiling lights, indirect lighting, cove lighting, rope or tape lighting, to name a few. There are even fixtures that beam light from the floor. This can be a tricky and unusual way to light residential space. It takes good planning and a thorough knowledge of building materials, architecture, and construction. Keep in mind too that light needs to have subtle highs and lows. There can't be any obvious shifts and, in my view, certainly no dark areas, which tend to bring a room down. I always insist on what I call a whisper of light in areas you don't intend to highlight.

The potential impact of decorative lighting is shown by a pivoting swing-arm sconce with drum shade (*left*) and a brass floor lamp with leaf-shaped fixtures (*right*). Design by Pavarini Design, Inc. *Photograph: © Marco Ricca Studio*

Layered sources brighten this living room: recessed white LED tape lights wash the face of the fireplace surround, a large-scale standing lamp illuminates one corner of the room, and a pair of table lamps ensure that no area is in shadow. RGB tape lighting brings color to the plaster ceiling and accentuates the form of the pierced-crown molding. An adjustable downlight illuminates sculpture on the console. Design by Pavarini Design, Inc. *Photographer: Dan Eifert*

In this dramatic view of a living room's ornamental plaster ceiling, there is RGB-LED cove lighting, recessed spot lighting, and a decorative chandelier whose translucent drum shade expands the scale of the fixture. Design by Pavarini Design, Inc. *Photographer: Dan Eifert*

Layering Light

There are various ways to fulfill a room's lighting needs, not all of them ideal. For example, you could say, "Well, we just put up eight recessed fixtures, so the room is fully lit." Lit, yes, but is the lighting layered? Does it truly define and enhance the interior space? Does it accentuate anything within the space, utilizing light and shadow to define its nuances, the forms within the room, or its style?

In this same vein, I'm always aware of how light is aimed into a room. Is it directed from a shaded sconce that's giving the room a soft glow? Is it an overhead fixture that's creating a wash of downlight directed toward the floor area? Is it defined by any type of cove lighting or backlighting?

This deserves repeating: If you're aiming to create a successful lighting scheme, you can't light a room from just one source or one direction—overheads or recessed fixtures. That creates a boring space, flat and uninteresting. Lighting a room only with sconces won't work either. Nor will a room be appropriately lit just by lamps. You will find that spending time in a room that has only one source of light, or light from only one direction, will feel one-dimensional and also induce fatigue. Good lighting expands your awareness of light and your perception of form, texture, and color in a room. Lighting done properly keeps you alert; it serves to hold you in that space. It makes the space feel welcoming and invites people to move into it. Invariably, too, it establishes a mood that can then enhance the designated function—a party mood, for example.

Factor in furnishings. In a living room, a cocktail table is a significant element because it defines the conversation zone. The area itself can be square, circular, or rectangular, depending on the seating composition. If the conversation area is lit by lamps, the coffee table may be in shadow or dimly lit. However, it should be lit in some manner because it is a place to display beautiful decorative objects or serve food and drinks.

A decorative urn is up-lit from an adjustable recessed floor fixture. Design by Pavarini Design, Inc. *Photograph: J. Randall Tarasuk*

6000K 2000K

In a kitchen's daytime view (*left*), the LED lighting is tuned to cool white (6000K). At night (*right*), the same space is tuned to warm-white LEDs (2000K). *Photo courtesy of PureEdge Lighting*

Recessed adjustable spotlights and RGB-LED cove lighting illuminate a finished interior. Design by Pavarini Design, Inc. *Photograph: Dan Eifert*

If it's possible to penetrate the living-room ceiling, I like to focus a little pinspot so the cocktail table receives its own subtle light. An MR-16 halogen or MR-16 LED would be appropriate. Each can bounce light off a surface or focus it onto the ceiling or directly into the room. If you can't penetrate the ceiling, try other means: for example, candles set on the coffee table or faux candles fired by batteries. Firelight, too, can give the table area emphasis.

Accent lighting must have a purpose. Is there a painting or decorative object that deserves to be highlighted, an element around which your room design will revolve? If it's a painting or framed work of art to be hung on the wall, you could opt for LED picture lights or a type of halogen developed specifically to light artwork. LEDs produce minimal heat and, lacking ultraviolet rays, will not fade colors.

In a lighting-concepts elevation drawing, the focus is on the design intent behind the placement of cove lighting and recessed adjustable spotlights.

An adjustable recessed spotlight's beam illuminates a crystal geode under a glass-topped cocktail table. Design by Pavarini Design, Inc. *Photograph: J. Randall Tarasuk*

An LED picture light washes a 6-foot-tall painting from top to bottom. Design by Pavarini Design, Inc. *Photograph: Phillip Ennis*

In an Asian-themed room, a collection of artifacts is displayed in decorative wall niches lit by recessed LED puck lights. *Photo courtesy of Sabrina Balsky Interior Design*

Halogens, similar in structure to traditional incandescents, are the only lighting sources that render color almost perfectly. However, because they get so hot, you'll need to install a UV filter to protect any artwork. While halogens were the standard for lighting art years ago, now LEDs have overtaken them because they remain cool and will not damage pigments.

Architectural elements or other details can be hit with a wash of light so they become a true focal point. This can be achieved with an adjustable recessed fixture that produces wide-beamed illumination from a halogen or LED fixture. Obvious examples would be a fireplace and mantel, along with any flanking bookcases.

Adjustable Trimless

An adjustable recessed light, set in its own housing, can be angled in different ways, depending on how a designer wishes to focus the light. *Photo courtesy of Amerlux Lighting Solutions*

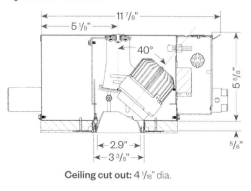

Ceiling cut out: 4 1/16" dia.

AMERLUX

A bookcase built into this living-room wall is traced by LED-integrated lighting that washes the contents of each shelf. Design by David Kleinberg. *Photograph: Phillip Ennis*

If installing fixtures in the ceiling is impractical, mount them on the apron below the crown molding, using picture lights that wash the whole installation. Or you could mount strip lights inside, on each cabinet stile. You would notch out the end corners on the front of every shelf so that a continuous lighting strip could be installed. Before LEDs and the availability of LED strips, we would have had to make do with what's known as incandescent click strips—tiny lightbulbs that snap into an electrical track vertically. The result was that all of the shelves would receive light and be illuminated evenly.

This was not always entirely satisfactory, because many bookcases lack stiles substantial enough to hide those strips. With LEDs, however, you would just need to make tiny shelving notches so that each strip could be hidden.

Another option is to design and install cabinets with clear-glass shelving. If the fixtures are properly mounted, light will cascade down from shelf to shelf, blocked only by the items displayed. Halogens or LEDs are ideal in this application; they make glass or crystal really sparkle.

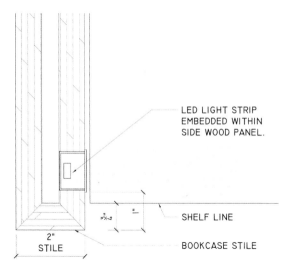

LED LIGHT STRIP
EMBEDDED WITHIN
SIDE WOOD PANEL.

SHELF LINE

2"
STILE

BOOKCASE STILE

This is how interior LED strip lighting was installed to respond to the bookcase profile while illuminating what each shelf displays.

Decorative lighting is a related concept in which the fixtures themselves provide the accents: pendant lights, sconces, table lamps, and standing lamps. They create those whispers of light I mentioned that prevent the room from having dark holes. To me, the dark holes are extremely disturbing, particularly if most of the room is lit beautifully.

Decorative lighting underscores the style of a room, not only by the fixtures but the way in which they emit light. Are there up-lights, for example? Does light come from openings in the front of the fixture, or does it wash down on the wall? In addition to complementing the forms and shapes in the room, decorative lighting creates its own light forms and shapes.

Proper lighting can also define specific areas. Think of a fixture hung between two club chairs and a small table. That arrangement and the light above it delineate a particular zone or setting and connote the specific function—perhaps conversational—intended for that space. For example, if we hang a light over a card table or a puzzle table, we are emphasizing a particular activity. Note that in a modern living room, we would not likely install a hanging fixture, as we would in a traditional or transitional-style interior.

We would want to keep the space clean and spare and depend on the placement of recessed lighting or nearby table lamps, as needed, to light that area.

Make sure the layers are balanced. This requires determining how much light will emanate from the different light sources. How much light will sconces emit? How about task lighting, which is often overlooked in a living room. After all, conversation is a task, and one of a living room's primary functions is to encourage

Lighted glass shelves illuminate the objects placed on them. *Photo courtesy of KLUS*

conversation. It is important not only to clearly see the person you're talking to, but to view them in flattering light, without shadows. Providing floor or table lamps in relationship to seating areas will enable you to illuminate your designated conversation area. I like to install a small-diameter recessed light above a cocktail table, which is the axis and focal point of a seating area.

All of these aspects of lighting should blend seamlessly from one light to the next, with no apparent breaks in illumination. When we see such a break, we are experiencing a dip into nonlight, which is shadow and sometimes darkness. So lighting needs to be layered and overlaid. The quality and intensity of the light can vary in brightness, but the whole room should be fully lit. Whenever we are sitting or standing, we need to be able to experience the entire space.

Keep in mind, however, that an evenly lit room can feel monotonous. Ideal lighting is what contains you so you feel visually comfortable in the space—and attractive. And in an attractive atmosphere, the balance of light should be readily apparent. If it doesn't exist, you might feel some discomfort without knowing precisely why. Sometimes that discomfort takes the form of fatigue.

Improper or inadequate room lighting is almost guaranteed to create fatigue.

Mood Making

Mood is a major component of living-space comfort, and I think any mood should be changeable, mainly through dimming, which is now described as lighting controls (see chapter 11, "True Tech"). With today's various lighting-control systems, you can set your light at a choice of levels. You can press a button and say to

Anyone using a keypad will have access to a variety of lighting moods, eliminating the need for banks of switches on the wall. *Photo courtesy of Lutron Electronics Co.*

yourself, "Okay, this is my cocktail-hour setting," and all the lights will shift to the level you specify, a preset that will create the feeling of an evening cocktail hour. Or it could be a party atmosphere or lighting appropriate to just sitting by the fire. Note that you can create a sensual mood in a room simply by altering the level of light. Adjusting light levels can create different feelings and other moods as well.

Light really does evoke emotions. For example, if you look at a color and it happens to be one you don't particularly like, you'll react with a particular feeling. You will respond differently, of course, if you happen to love that color. I think people react to light in parallel ways, which is why I consistently use light to underscore the mood of intimacy in an interior room setting. I consider it just as important as color and texture, because good lighting has the ability to actually enhance color and texture—and make people feel good too. For me, light is always an essential design tool.

Here's an example from some time back, when designers lacked the option of using other than traditional incandescent bulbs. My firm was challenged to light the library of a Tenafly, New Jersey, home that was all intricately paneled. Paneled rooms tend to be dark, of course, so our solution was to install lighting that would effectively wash the draperies. They were sheer with a slight shimmer, which contrasted well with the unavoidable dullness and flatness of the wood. Tackling that installation today, we would opt for an LED strip because it would generate less heat than incandescent strip lighting and thus could be installed closer to the fabric.

Adding this perception of depth made the room feel more interesting. That's what good lighting does. It helps us perceive depth and texture much more fully. If, for example, a living room has upholstered furniture with great texture, your eye might not acknowledge that texture but perceive the fabric mainly as being flat. Good lighting will bring out that texture; however, even just a whisper of light will do the same.

Focal Points

I once designed a large living room with 12-foot ceilings for a house on West 74th Street in Manhattan. There were no moldings or casings; the room was basically a white box devoid of architectural interest. To create a focal point, I acquired an important piece of art, lighting it with a halogen spotlight, adjustable within 30 degrees and mounted at an angle of about 45 degrees from the ceiling. Yes, I could have put up a work of art without any spotlighting, but it would

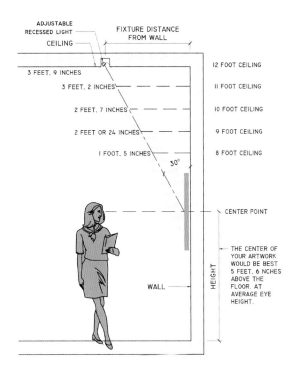

This diagram shows the appropriate placement of ceiling lights to illuminate objects

not have commanded any particular attention. That's what accent lighting does; it draws the eye to what you want people to focus on.

Instead of hanging a painting, I mounted a massive porcelain ginger jar on a bracket against the fireplace wall. I told the clients, "We'll need to install a special light, so we can actually experience the form of the piece and make it a focal point in the room." At first they resisted, knowing they would have to trench through the ceiling to get light to the proper location. This would be a costly installation because later, of course, they would have to repair the ceiling.

"What else can we do?" they wondered. "Can't we just put a light on the floor?" No. I knew that wouldn't work, not there. Light needs to have its own proper direction.

The ginger jar was probably 22 inches tall, and it had a teal glaze. This was a piece I had acquired especially for my clients because I knew it would pull color from some of the fabrics we had chosen. Would it have been a focus if we hadn't given particular attention to lighting it? Probably not. It would have been just a colored shape up on the wall, nothing more. But with its own special light, it could achieve real prominence, adding to the room's interest and drama. After much discussion, my clients acquiesced and ultimately were glad they had.

When something is lit in a special way, your eye will always be drawn to it, just as it would be in a theatrical production whose director has determined what the audience should focus on. This is what spotlights do. Sitting in a theater, we direct our attention to what the creators want us to look at. Similarly, in designing an interior, the architect or the designer of the space will want to direct our eyes to what we should see and experience. It might be a painting, acquired pottery, or sculpture, or it could be some other object or even a piece of furniture. To achieve the needed emphasis, a designer will usually accentuate the object with light.

I recall a living room my firm designed in a Park Avenue apartment. It had a high ceiling—about 14 feet—that was absolutely flat, with typical crown molding along the periphery. After some investigation and a thorough probing, we proposed a solution: raise the ceiling about 18 inches and create a vault, add plaster moldings, and leave a soffit around the periphery to house the mechanicals. Of course the client first wondered, "Why do we have to do all that? Why do we have to assume the expense of putting light in the cove when we have the ability to illuminate that ceiling from other light sources below?"

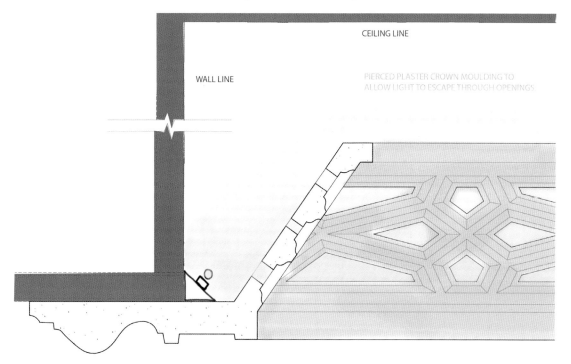

CEILING LINE

WALL LINE

PIERCED PLASTER CROWN MOULDING TO ALLOW LIGHT TO ESCAPE THROUGH OPENINGS

Crown molding was pierced to allow LED strip lights mounted behind it to projects subtle light beams onto the ceiling and into the room. Design by Pavarini Design, Inc. *Photograph: © Marco Ricca Studio*

We ultimately convinced the client that a different experience could be created when light comes from above, rather than only from lamps and sconces placed throughout the room. We crafted a little mockup fixture to put in the cove, and when our client saw that, the whole room came alive for them—and for me as well. Grasping what the potential effect would be, the wife said, "Oh, my God, do it!"

Raising that ceiling 18 inches gave us the ability to position the crown up into that elevated area and the molding we had developed. Then by designing a pierced plaster crown, we knew we could shine light not only up, onto the ceiling, but also deep into the room itself, with either cold cathodes, LEDs, or incandescent bulbs. LEDs ended up being our choice, not only because of their longevity but also because they send light in all directions—in this case, bouncing it off the inside wall: up, down, and to the back. We installed detailed plasterwork on the new ceiling, which we could then illuminate effectively to heighten the visual experience of being in that room. This was a subtle, but significant, addition to the room's lighting plan. Note that I'm never interested in making people aware of the source of light in a room, only in the effect the light source has on the overall experience of being in that room.

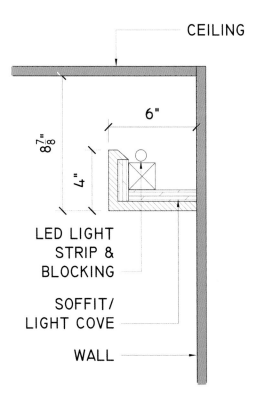

CEILING

6"

$8\frac{7}{8}$"

4"

LED LIGHT
STRIP &
BLOCKING

SOFFIT/
LIGHT COVE

WALL

Placement of LED lighting in a ceiling cove will succeed if the fixtures are as close as possible to the upper edge of the cove.

More about Balance

Personally, I don't like putting a recessed overhead in a living room. For me, that fixture would never create a particularly flattering light—unless it happens to be an accent light emanating from the ceiling or from any of those areas that receive whispers of light. Instead, I favor installing sconces at the fireplace or accent light on a painting above the mantel. At the other end of the room there may be some seating, and, if so, between the fireplace and that seating arrangement, there should be a whisper of light. Its purpose would be to prevent deep shadows or patches of darkness from occurring.

To achieve that whisper of light, I would install a small, adjustable recessed fixture, one with a tiny aperture, or opening, behind which there could be an LED that's only an inch in diameter. What you want to produce is simply a glow, so you're not shifting from a well-lit fireplace elevation to darkness leading to your seating area. What you're trying to avoid are those severe dips in light level that can be so disturbing—they absolutely shatter any mood you're trying to sustain. That's why I consider balance so important.

Another challenging project involved a two-bedroom apartment in a relatively recent building on Manhattan's Madison Avenue, a contemporary design with predictably low ceilings. Since the living room was large, our challenge was finding a way to shine light into the middle of the space. We knew we couldn't achieve that effectively from overheads, because the ceiling was solid concrete (always know your architecture).

Because the floor of this apartment, like its ceiling, was also a concrete slab, we could see that there was no way to install floor outlets or recessed lights. All our lighting had to be placed around the perimeter. How about running wires under carpeting? Not possible here. That would have violated code, and, of course, we weren't planning to lay carpeting anyway.

After giving the plan much thought, we decided to drop the ceiling slightly, just along the perimeter, so we could install cove lighting—in this case, LED strips to wash the center of that surface. Then to make sure we could bounce light effectively, we chose a ceiling treatment that would create a reflective sheen. It delivered light to the center of the room, where, without proper outlets, it would not have been possible to light effectively with floor lamps or table lamps.

Not only did we include cove lighting in that room, to direct lighting up, toward the ceiling, we also punctured the cove in key locations. We wanted to make sure that some accent lighting could also be directed down, highlighting those decorative elements we felt deserved to receive special emphasis.

Note that when you create a ceiling plan, the lights should not be positioned randomly. Some kind of geometry must be adhered to, if overheads will be used to light the space. Personally, I would want to see all the lights properly aligned, so that when you look up at the ceiling, there is some order to the placement—it should not be a random arrangement that could create visual chaos on the ceiling.

The Versatility Challenge

Unlike a dining room or a bedroom, spaces designed mainly to fulfill a single purpose, a living room should be versatile. How do we make it so? Mainly by creating different layers of light—or zones of light—from standing lamps, table lamps, sconces, and maybe one or more fixtures overhead. Using sophisticated

dimmers—now referred to as lighting controls (see chapter 11, "True Tech")—we can also design the light to create different moods with prescribed settings (scenic modes, for example). Adjusting light levels can alter both the quality and quantity of light within a space, but controlling the light doesn't just involve dimming it. For example, if detailed work is contemplated for a particular space, especially a living room, you will want the ability to actually raise the accent-lighting level there.

Color and Placement

In addition to focusing our attention, light alters our perception of color, even when that color is white. A swatch of orange fabric looks different under artificial light than in daylight. Therefore it's logical to wonder how the presence of daylight may change the way you deal with color. Keep in mind, though, that a living room is more likely to be experienced

In a living room, soft sheer drapery panels and woven wooden shades combine to achieve a soothing effect by diffusing the sunlight. Design by Pavarini Design, Inc. *Photograph: Doug Holt Photography*

at night than in daytime, which means the space should be designed mostly for use under artificial light. Even if it is used during the day to host luncheons and the like, well-designed window coverings will mediate the sunlight.

Another point to remember: glare is always an issue, and I am particularly sensitive to it. I become deeply irritated when light is pouring down on me from a high angle. If I'm seated at a restaurant where light is shining in my eyes from above, I will ask to be moved. Light in a living room should be relatively soft. You want the light to come from the side; it just feels better when you're at the same level as your light source, which may be why so many people light a living room with decorative lamps.

Lighting Step by Step

1. Define the room's purpose(s). Knowing what "living" in this room actually entails will guide your decision-making. The idea of "living" may seem obvious, but it can be interpreted in different ways, and its use will vary, depending on your or your clients' priorities, needs, and preferences. To create a successful "lightscape," knowing how the room is be used will help you build the kind of layered light that points up the impact of your interior design.

2. Identify or create the focal points you can enhance with light. Multiple focal points make a room more interesting. I like it when I stand in a room and as I turn, there is something on each elevation that grabs my attention. It could be color or the finish on the color. It could be a decorative object or the way a window treatment folds. It might also be draperies that vary the perception of light coming in. It could also be the material on the face of the fireplace, a painting, or even the frame of a painting.

3. Consider the middle layer of light, which falls somewhere between ambient and task or accent lighting. Its purpose is to create interest without visually shifting the emphasis from key focal points. Use of this middle layer needs to be seamless, which means you can't shift abruptly from a high to a low.

4. Create lighting that's washed on a major piece of furniture, perhaps an antique. The light level could be a tiny bit brighter, a little more intense than the room's general lighting. It should provide interest in specific areas without detracting from focal points.

5. Fill in the areas that appear dark in your plan. This layer of light should be soft, though not as soft as that whisper of light I referred to earlier or as bright as your lighting's middle level. The idea is to light any possible dark areas, such as where the living room opens into a hallway. Avoid an abrupt shift from dim to bright light anywhere in the house.

Unifying Fixtures

An essential aspect of lighting a living room or any interior space is choosing the fixtures. How do you unify them? Mainly by whatever finish you select—important, because decorative fixtures can pinpoint styles. Your choices include various metals, wood tones, and colors in the fixtures themselves. Or if you prefer to include a variety of light fixtures, choose similar styles and also similar materials for your shades. When you place light behind a lampshade, the light will appear to be filtered—that's a lampshade's purpose, of course.

And when choosing your lampshades, keep in mind that if they project pools of light onto the ceiling, you'll want them to be similar in color temperature. Otherwise the light pools on that ceiling will have different color intensities—an unattractive mix.

One special caveat: In designing a large living room, if you order several lampshades in a neutral tone and abruptly include a black paper shade, even if only as an accent, you'll find you've made the room start to tip. Talk about balance of light and tone in a room! That's why you'll want to make sure the whole room seems to be on one level—one area not lit more than any other—so the room will not appear to sink on one side. If not, you'll actually seem to feel it tilting!

There's a subtlety in lighting a living room successfully. You do have focal points; you do have fixtures; you do have highs and lows (I don't mean dark, of course). If the lighting is subtly designed and creatively executed, the room will come alive because you've made it interesting. Good lighting will bring out texture. It will also bring out form, each of which is at the heart of any room design.

Living-Room Tips

• Consider your main light source: chandelier, pendant, or surface-mounted fixture. Then look to the room's perimeter for additional lighting.

• Access the natural-light orientation of the room but make sure the space can be well lit after the sunlight has faded and the room is readied for evening use.

• Make sure potentially dark corners are adequately lit, but allow some dimmer areas, so the room has some darker, quieter "moments."

• Without a measure of light contrast, the room will seem flat and uninteresting. The subtle interplay of dark, light, and shadow will give the room depth and interest.

• To expand visual interest even more, mix it up: layer the room with different light sources.

• Specify light sources that are 2700K to 3000K, and keep in mind that frosted or soft-white bulbs will soften the glare from any unshielded light source.

• Avoid using excessive amounts of overhead lighting; it will create bright spots in the ceiling and unwanted shadows below. Ideally, a living-room ceiling plane should be clean—with no holes!

• Turn lampshades so that no seams are exposed, especially when fixtures are lit.

• Always determine the size of your tape lighting before you start to construct or install anything.

• For complete flexibility, be sure all the lighting is on dimmers. This will allow you to create different levels of light to focus on different areas, when needed.

• A useful way to provide ambient lighting in a living room is to wash the walls with light. Use a soffit valance and, to enhance the room's architecture, valance lighting.

• I often reverse the lighting in crowns by affixing each crown far enough away from the wall to provide space to house an LED strip tape. Its light will graze downward on the wall; this is particularly effective when walls are faced with murals, decorative paint, or illustrative paper.

Recessed linear lighting created an opportunity for the lighting in a contemporary interior to function as a component of the design scheme. TruLine recessed linear lighting criss-crosses the walls and ceilings of a living space, creating a dazzling composition. A standing lamp balances the composition, rather than dominating the room's illumination. *Photo courtesy of PureEdge Lighting*

Recessed fixtures, standing lamps, table lamps, and a chandelier combine with cove lights to achieve a complete lighting scheme—layered illumination in a luxe dining room. Design by Pavarini Design, Inc. *Photograph: © Marco Ricca Studio*

CHAPTER 4
The Functional but Flexible Dining Room

Even a single lamp dispels the deepest darkness.
—Mahatma Gandhi, political ethicist

Proper lighting is absolutely critical in a dining room, probably more so than in any other room. It's how you create an atmosphere, and that atmosphere is what really shapes a dining event. Even if formal entertaining is to occur there, in most homes today, dining rooms are flexible spaces rather than dedicated to occasional dinner guests. Before I begin making sketches, I try to get a clear picture of how this room is likely to be lived in.

Many people use their dining table as a desk or a place where their kids can sit and do homework. Others like to enjoy a cup of coffee—and perhaps read a newspaper or use their iPAD or laptop—while seated alone at the head of the table. When clients tell me they want a flexible dining room, it doesn't mean the furniture should be on wheels so it can be moved around. I believe the placement of a dining table and chairs should be fixed but its capacity should be flexible—expanded as needed by adding leaves in the center or at the ends. No matter how that table expands, it's the core of a setup that's not going to move, so the lighting can be considered a permanent solution too.

Because a dining room typically gets more use after dark, my approach to lighting is more dramatic than in other rooms. The dining table is the likely focus, and so I favor low-level lighting to add intimacy to a setting in which people are looking across the table at one another.

In some situations, I may install two overhead lights so that the table can still be lit effectively when it is expanded. I would choose a pair of 2-inch-square-or-round LEDs, each registering 2700K with a color-rendering index (CRI) of 95 or more, and place them halfway between the midpoint of the table and each end. The ceiling openings would be so small that, once installed, those tiny LED fixtures would achieve the *effect* of light, without the glare resulting from incandescent bulbs in 6-to-8-inch openings. Another disadvantage with openings that big is that the light source is visible even when the lights are off.

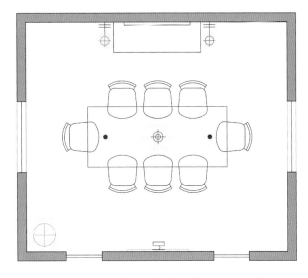

Lighting concepts complete a furniture floor plan that illustrates how an entire tabletop can be skillfully lit by one chandelier and two recessed fixtures.

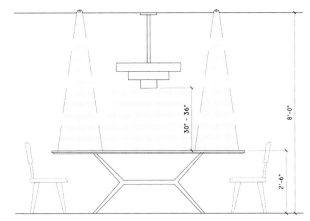

Critical dimensions on a dining-room elevation plan include room height and the distance between the bottom of the chandelier and the table surface.

A pair of LED chandeliers with additional layered lighting completes a successful lighting scheme.

Creating an Atmosphere

You want to create an atmosphere in which the rest of the room recedes. The focus is the table and the diners. However, no matter what the table configuration—expanded or compressed—the lighting should be conceived as a whole. This means having multiple light sources such as lamps and sconces on dimmers. For example, low light is flattering, reassuring, and sexy. It creates a feeling of intimacy at a formal dinner, but for a less formal occasion or family meal, the room should be brighter. (For a roundup of lighting controls and how to apply them, see chapter 11, "True Tech.")

Several years ago, my team and I designed a dining room for a Manhattan couple who wanted it to seat at least fourteen people. The space measured roughly 16 by 20 feet; the table we chose was 10 feet long and could be expanded for special occasions. We knew that one light fixture over the table would be insufficient, so we installed two chandeliers about 4 feet apart and added standing lamps in two corners of the room, plus a lighting cove over the credenza we had placed against one wall.

If we were doing such a room today, I would specify LEDs, paying careful attention to the bulbs' color temperature and CRI to keep the room from feeling cold. Some lighting consultants routinely specify 3000K for residential use, but I think that is too cool. I'd opt for a slightly warm glow—around 2700K, so that those seated at the table look their best and the food looks appetizing.

Wherever the dining table and chairs are placed is where the room's activities will probably occur. However, a buffet sideboard could also become a backup cabinet for a desk, a place to stack books, binders, papers, and perhaps a laptop or an iPad.

Three staggered hanging pendants cast light through a perforated table base, projecting patterns on the floor for visual effect. LED cove lighting provides ambient indirect lighting. Design by Francis Toumbakaris. *Photograph: Edward Caruso Photography*

In that case, rather than installing a hanging fixture over the dining table, I would use a diffused surface-mount ceiling fixture to supply the essential ambient light. If a dining-room ceiling happens to be made of concrete, as it often is in new apartment construction, we will apply a layer of ⅝-inch-thick Sheetrock to the surface and install LED lighting inside it. This arrangement allows a delicate ribbon of light to be projected down, directly in front of where people will be sitting or standing, and avoids putting anyone in shadow. An alternative to chipping into a concrete surface is to create cove or soffit lighting.

Another approach is to light the room with candles. Dining by candlelight is something people really enjoy. While designing a penthouse apartment in a Park Avenue building, I learned that Brooke Astor, the late, great philanthropist and society matron, had lived two floors below. She was gone by then, but her apartment was still intact, pending its eventual sale. My client was eager for me to see it.

In a minimalist dining area, the space is lit only by PureEdge Truline LED strips integrated into the Sheetrock on the walls and ceiling to frame the area in light. Three recessed lights spotlight the center of the table. *Photo courtesy of PureEdge Lighting*

In a traditional dining room, antique candelabra were electrified to provide ample lighting and ambience to the opulent table setting. Diaphanous custom lampshades were fitted to the candelabra to diffuse the light and bring another layer to the decor. Design by Pavarini Design, Inc. *Photo by Phillip Ennis*

Mrs. Astor's dining room was probably 60 feet long, big enough for a table that could seat at least forty people. I noticed, however, that there was no provision for lighting other than the picture lights that illuminated the antique wall murals she curated. How did she light those incredible dinner-table settings for which she was so famous? Only with candles, I learned—dozens and dozens arranged down the length of the table. Sitting there in that light must have been a mind-altering experience—in a word, mystical.

Short candles in small holders illuminate only what's immediately around them on either side of the table. Long candles in a tall candelabra will light much more of the room. That's really why candelabra were developed. Using candles or gas fixtures, it was always possible to look directly into the flame and perhaps be transfixed by it. By comparison, electric lighting proved much too intense; it had to be shaded to temper the glare, giving rise to a multitude of lampshade designs.

In an ultramodern design, there might not be any kind of decorative fixture; thus candlelight would be an ideal choice. But if the ceiling can be penetrated, recessed lighting is a plausible alternative. Using LEDs, you almost never see where ceiling light originates because the fixtures are so small. This shrinking bulb size is another example of the rapid pace of today's home lighting refinements. In one dining room we designed, we were able to summon an incredible volume of light from a recessed fixture that was only an inch and a half in diameter. When switched off, the fixtures were barely visible. The beauty of such an arrangement is that it avoids creating holes that make a ceiling resemble a slice of Swiss cheese—an effect known in the lighting industry as "ceiling acne."

Multiple Light Modes

A similar kind of ingenuity was involved in another Manhattan dining room. We couldn't install any kind of overhead fixture because there was no electrical box in the ornate plaster ceiling. There was an outlet on the floor, however. The solution to this challenge—which became a major design element—was to place two magnificent lamps on the table, each one plugged into the floor outlet. That was the only way to get ambient light where we needed it. By installing table lamps on the dining table, we addressed both the functional and the decorative aspects of the project, and in a way that was visually pleasing.

iGuzzini Blade microrecessed LEDs were installed in this ceiling. Design by Pavarini Design, Inc. *Photograph: Phillip Ennis*

Laser Blade XS "The Blade"

1 1/8"

iGuzzini

The LED in hand, an iGuzzini Laser Blade XS LED labeled "The Blade," measures only 1⅛ inches. *Photo courtesy of iGuzzini illuminazione*

In lieu of chandeliers, a lavishly scaled dining room is lit indirectly by LED cove lighting. The equipment has been tucked into the crown molding to provide general illumination that, through the use of color-changing RGB LED lighting, also adds festive flair to the exuberant interior space. Design by Pavarini Design, Inc. *Photo by Phillip Ennis*

Some dining rooms double as a music room. More than one client has said, "I want to put my baby grand piano at the end of the room, near the bay window." A piano requires both ambient lighting and task lighting so the music on the tilted stand can be read. In a Connecticut home, we were challenged to light a piano in a space where the music rack received virtually no light. Because the clients didn't want us to install overhead fixtures, we chose a standing task lamp with an arm at the appropriate height. This was a much-better choice than a clip-on light for the music rack or a table lamp placed far forward on the piano. Most important, the light source was dimmable and barely perceptible.

A standing piano lamp can be positioned to illuminate the keyboard as well as the music rack above it. *Photo courtesy of House of Troy Lighting*

I am convinced that all lighting in a home should be dimmable. Available now are "tunable" white LEDs that are not only dimmable but adjustable from a warm to neutral to cool color (see chapter 11, "True Tech").

A dining room might also include a cocktail bar in one corner or against a wall. If the bar is a stand-up space, ambient lighting should be sufficient. But if there are stools for people to sit on while they sip a drink, the surface in front of them needs a focused light. The same is true whether a surface is used for eating, reading, or doing jigsaw puzzles. Light is employed to enhance our perception of space and form, and also to help us perform tasks associated with everyday living.

When a dining room flows out of an open kitchen, or the kitchen has a breakfast-bar extension, lighting it helps define the space. What will underscore the separation of one area from another is the quality, color, and level of light. This is a much more interesting approach than creating a physical barrier.

In some situations we might install a hanging fixture that distinguishes the breakfast-bar end of the counter from the working end. For ambient and task lighting, I often install a trough for LED tape light in the ceiling above the counter, following the counter's shape. This provides better illumination than typical recessed downlights because it doesn't interrupt the flow of light.

Until the advent of LEDs, I would not have been able to do something so subtle yet so wonderfully effective! They have made me think more creatively and consider vastly different ways of employing light. The LED is such a flexible product that it can be used in countless ways by anyone who is knowledgeable, confident, and creative enough to take advantage of its potential.

Dining rooms, like any rooms lit with LEDs, will inevitably look cleaner and more modern than the old incandescent lighting, and the lighting may feel out of place in a traditional setting. For example, after I delivered a lecture on lighting recently, a designer friend approached me, shaking his head. "I just lit a client's huge bookshelf, and when I threw the switch on, I realized the lighting was all wrong," he confessed. He had specified LED lighting, but without knowledge of what type of light to use or how to install it. He ended up with a setup that, he said, "really looked awful." The focus was wrong, the color temperature was too cool, the nodes were not adequately diffused, and the CRI was too low. In effect, what he'd produced was not doing anything even close to what he thought it would do.

The thing to keep in mind when faced with these dilemmas is that LEDs are flexible enough to integrate into almost any application because their light quality can be controlled. However, you might need a professional to help you achieve the lighting effect you desire.

The way we work with light now is more cerebral and thought provoking than ever in project design, execution, and intent. Without a doubt, it allows us to make light a major component of design—a true design tool.

Dining-Room Tips

• Make a statement! A dining room benefits from a sense of drama.

• Base your lighting on the location of the dining table.

• For a one-of-a-kind look, use multiple pendant lights in odd numbers over the table.

• In an open-plan space or a merged kitchen-dining area, a large pendant light over the table can be a zoning aid. Even in daylight, a large pendant focuses the eye on the table, dividing the eating zone from the rest of the room.

• Use dimmers to control the mood and flatter guests.

• Layer light with table lamps, standing lamps, and sconces. Table, desk, and floor lamps can be shifted to give your lighting plan even greater flexibility.

• Use 2700K in all light fixtures for an even color distribution.

• If you choose fixtures—chandelier, sconces, or lamps—that expose the light source, install frosted bulbs to soften the glare.

• When installing a chandelier, the bottom of the light fixture should be 30 to 36 inches above the table, a calculation that, of course, doesn't take into consideration the light's type, density, or style. While rules must be learned, they can also be broken, if necessary, to makes a unique design statement.

• If the style of the room warrants lampshades, make them unique—be open to something different.

Polished stainless-steel crown molding with integrated LED lighting and a decorative glass chandelier make a statement in this modern dining room. Design by Pavarini Design, Inc. *Photographer: J. Randall Tarasuk*

The All-Purpose Family Room

Lighting is everything. It creates atmosphere, drama, and intrigue in a room.
—Martin Lawrence Bullard, interior designer

This room is the true hub of a home, the spot where everyone tends to gather for a variety of activities. They're on their computers or their iPads, reading books or playing board games, watching TV, listening to music, or having conversations. Sometimes they are also entertaining guests.

Consider a family room intimate space. Depending on the size of the room or the household structure, there could be different zones for different activities. Or, some functions could be combined—board games set up on a cocktail table, for example, instead of a separate game table.

What's the Plan?

Before the room is wired and lighted, you have to know exactly how it will be used—what furniture will be chosen, where it will all go, and how each piece will relate to the others. If room furnishings are to include a TV, to light it properly you need to know where it will be placed. If you place the seating in the center of the room rather than along the periphery, you'll need to consider where to install floor outlets. If you have access to wire from below (with new construction, you always have this ability), you won't end up with a cord from a table lamp crossing the floor and plugging into a wall (you should just not do that!).

Overall, a family room should be considered informal space. It should be inviting and comfortable, whether it's a place where close friends gather or is used as a private family retreat. Anything can happen in this room.

Layered lighting in a family room includes an ornamental chandelier, a pair of antique verdigris table lamps that light the center of the room, and a window-side table lamp whose beams illuminate a conversation area. Design by Pavarini Design, Inc. *Photograph: Doug Holt Photography*

A living room with recessed shelves is lit by linear LEDs and a trio of decorative pendants, setting a mood in this modern metropolitan home. Design by Francis Toumbakaris. *Photograph: Edward Caruso Photography*

Balancing Light

Regardless of a room's size, location, or potential use, we always start with the basics: ambient (or overall) lighting, task lighting, decorative lighting, and accent lighting. Successful lighting is layered with these four lighting concepts. They are our guideposts, and we approach them in whatever order seems appropriate for each project. In every instance, we keep in mind that what lighting does for us, beyond providing illumination, is direct our focus. It grabs our attention, compelling us to look at something.

To maintain the flexibility of this multipurpose space, you probably won't want to suspend light fixtures as permanent installations. Instead, consider recessed ceiling fixtures and wall sconces to create ambient lighting with optimum flexibility. Why? Because you never know when you may want to move a table, sofa, or armchair. So, think about installing sconces in key

areas—each with a glass, paper, or fabric shade—so their light beams project outward, into the core of the space. Where you place them depends on the room and your overall plan. To avoid a cluttered ceiling arrangement, I tend to design with as few recessed fixtures as possible.

Consider balanced light when formulating your plan. If the room has a fireplace, which many family rooms do, keep in mind that this is a true focal point and has always been, no matter what the period of the house.

Light is a powerful attraction, compelling one's vision to focus on whatever is illuminated.

A fireplace can be a significant focal point in a room's design, particularly when flanked by symmetrically placed sconces that lend harmony and balance.

Throughout history, we've always seen light emanating from lamps on the mantel or from sconces or candles flanking the fireplace. If you are placing sconces at either end of a mantel, consider balancing them by hanging another pair of sconces on the opposite wall. If there's too much light at one end, the room will feel heavy on that side and will seem to tilt.

This doesn't mean that all sconces must have an exact counterpoint. There's no reason you can't use sconces on one side and maybe table lamps on the other—or accent lights, even recessed ceiling fixtures. My point is this: you don't want to inadvertently create either lighting hotspots or dark, shadowy areas. Balanced light makes the space feel more interesting by expanding the perception of depth.

Ceiling Options

A great many family rooms have either a gabled or a pitched ceiling. In that situation, chandeliers might be a good source of overall light (they would not be if the ceiling was flat).

A cathedral ceiling is often defined by a different material—painted or stained wooden planks, for example. If it's a gabled ceiling, beams are often left exposed. What a great opportunity! In creating ambient light, why not use that architectural element as a way to light the ceiling by installing LED lighting along the top of each beam?

Because they're so small, LED strip lights relieve us of the need to find ways to hide the fixtures. No more than ¼ to ⅜ inch high, they are low-profile enough to

Monopoint fixtures were installed on top of the structural beam and were focused to bring ambient light to a room with a cathedral ceiling. Design by John Barman, Inc. *Photograph: Eric Laignel*

be installed across the upper surface of each beam, making them invisible from below. I would place these fixtures judiciously, being careful not to create any ceiling hotspots of light projected from either end of the beam. If the ceiling is to be painted, consider a tone that will bounce the light down into the room. However, even a natural or stained wooden surface will bounce some light down and add to the room's ambient lighting.

In a room with a pitched ceiling and no beams, you may want to install recessed fixtures. If so, avoid choosing just any recessed fixture, because the beam of light will be perpendicular to the sloped ceiling surface, resulting in an oddly angled beam spread. You can purchase adjustable fixtures designed for sloped ceilings, allowing the light beams to be perpendicular to the floor. With such units, I can shift the light within each housing either to angle into the room or to direct light straight down to the floor.

Another way to illuminate a pitched ceiling is to mount sconces on opposite walls. This will not only wash the ceiling with light but also create a bounce effect, directing light into the room. All lights have a defined beam spread—from the point where the light originates to the surface it hits. Ceiling height and potential beam spread will determine how your lights should be positioned.

I feel strongly that when creating a room's overall lighting, you don't want pools of light, with shadowed areas in between. The lighting should overlap, so that what reaches the floor is continuous light. Placement depends on answers to these questions: How high is the ceiling? What is the likely beam spread? Are you lighting a sofa, a framed piece of art, a table, or a console on the floor? Each scenario requires a slightly different calculation. And keep in mind that how far apart to place the ceiling fixtures, whether they are recessed lights or track lights, depends on the ceiling height. For instance, if you have lights with a 60-degree beam spread, you'll need to calculate what the overlap needs to be when the light beams reach the floor.

The Cove Advantage

Many newer homes have family rooms with built-in ceiling coves. The feature could be an soffit built out of Sheetrock or simply a crown molding—in wood, plaster, acrylic, or other material—that provides enough

Provocative lighting details can be attained with knife-edge extrusions with integrated LED lighting, making the ceiling / wall panel appear paper thin. *Photo courtesy of KLUS*

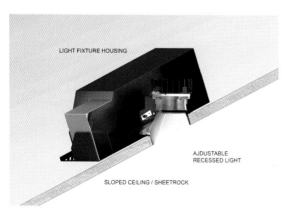

LIGHT FIXTURE HOUSING

AJDUSTABLE RECESSED LIGHT

SLOPED CEILING / SHEETROCK

In a cross section of a recessed LED light housing designed for sloped ceilings, note that the fixture's position can be adjusted according to how you want light aimed down into the room. *BeveLED Mini® Incline® for Sloped Ceilings by USAI® Lighting*

SCAN CODE

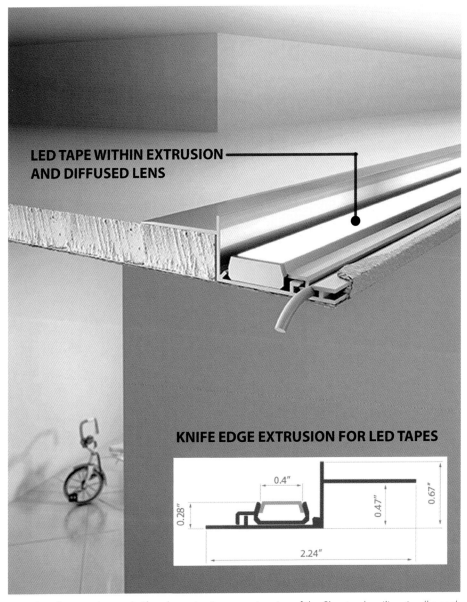

LED TAPE WITHIN EXTRUSION AND DIFFUSED LENS

KNIFE EDGE EXTRUSION FOR LED TAPES

0.4"

0.28"

0.47"

0.67"

2.24"

A section diagram shows a knife-edge extrusion, an extension of the Sheetrock ceiling / wall panel. Integrated with LED lighting, its low profile allows light to be embedded in architecture for seamless indirect illumination. *Photo courtesy of KLUS*

SCAN

CODE

KLUS

space to install an LED lighting strip and, perhaps, a diffuser. That strip is minuscule, maybe only ¼ inch thick or ⅜ inch high, but that's all you need—truly—and you'll find that you can get a lot of light out of it.

Precise light placement in a cove is key. Putting it deep within the cove will produce a band of light around the periphery of the room, plus a shadow. I find that I can get more light spread into the center of the ceiling by positioning fixtures in the upper part of the soffit or cove. I make sure the lights are almost even with the top of the cove, not thrust deep down into it, where some of their light would be trapped within the cove.

Focused Light for Effect

Luminaires are dependable types of decorative fixtures. When chosen for accent lighting, their use needs to be flexible—a word with multiple meanings in this context. If you're lighting a painting you've hung over a mantel, for example, you'll want that light to be adjustable, in case you decide to move or change the piece of art someday. You'll also want to be able to focus the light or angle it, no matter what you put above that mantel.

Here's my own improvised calculation: If the light is to originate some distance from the piece being lit, I'll probably use two luminaires. I have found that in similar situations, if the artwork is exceptionally large, I might not be able to light it appropriately with just one ceiling fixture. It may not have the capacity to illuminate the entire painting, which means I would get dark spots along one or more edges and a fade-out to shadow.

When illuminating art hung over a mantel, I usually opt for two adjustable fixtures, so I can cross their beams. And picture lights are not always appropriate because they tend to state, in effect, "This is a work of art!" Usually, in a family room—which is neither a gallery nor a museum display—you're hanging personal pieces, rather than artistic treasures, in groupings such as family photographs, children's first brushstrokes, or modest prints. In that setting, picture lights would just get in the way.

What's the alternative? LED lighting, which does the job without making a particular statement. And it's terrific for illuminating any work of art, because it doesn't fade pigment or project heat. Today's LED picture lights can illuminate up to 7 feet of painting height without creating shadows.

By contrast, if you happened to be using halogens, another popular long-burning source of light (see

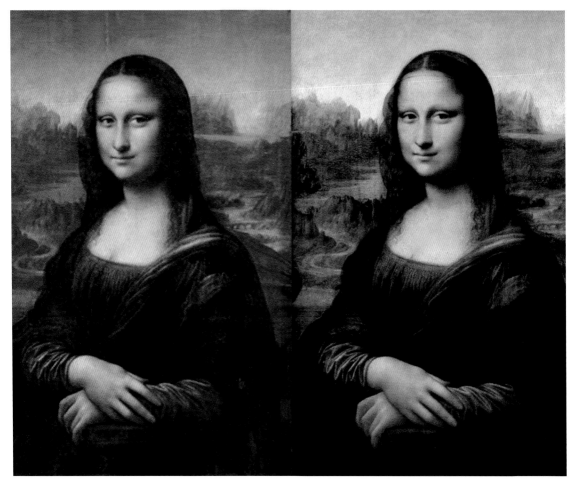

Leonardo da Vinci's iconic *Mona Lisa* is shown before (*left*) and after relamping with LEDs. Notice the clarity of the pigmentation when properly balanced LED lighting reveals the painting's true colors. *Photograph: J. Randall Tarasuk*

chapter 1, "A Light Look Ahead"), you'd find that the beam would not wash the entire surface of the painting. Instead, the light would just reach a certain point and then cut off, placing the rest of the work in shadow. Most important, halogens would be potentially damaging to photography and paintings, not only because of their extreme heat but also because of the UV rays they emit. LEDs are more art-friendly; they produce less heat and emit no damaging rays. The Louvre's famous Da Vinci *Mona Lisa* has been relit with LEDs.

In a family room, you're likely to have at least one wall devoted to informal images—snapshots, color portraits, children's work—all in frames of different materials and dimensions. Here, it would be especially important to focus on flexible lighting, so different arrangements can be accommodated over time.

Usually, the light directed at these informal picture walls will come from above, from track lights or fixtures recessed into the ceiling. For this task, I highly recommend adjustable focused LEDs or LED wall washers that will evenly supply overall wall lighting. You can achieve this effect with recessed lighting, if your ceiling allows it, or track lighting, if you're unable to penetrate the surface.

I don't care for fixtures whose apertures, when adjusted, extend below the ceiling plane. I prefer using fixtures with enough depth that their adjustability is concealed above the ceiling plane. There is nothing worse than entering a room and seeing recessed lighting fixtures dipping below the ceiling plane. To my mind, that would make the lighting, and even the room itself, feel quite dated, like those "eyeball" lights that were used widely in the late twentieth century.

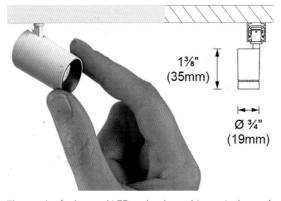

The result of advanced LED technology, this particular track fixture measures just ¾ by 1⅜ inches, making discreet installation possible. *Photo courtesy of iGuzzini illuminazione*

Tasks at Hand

What kind of task lighting will your family room require? That depends on the kind of activity that's likely to occur in that space. Do you plan to retreat there to use your phone or laptop, or to read a book, a magazine, or the latest download on your Kindle? Do you prefer curling up on a sofa or lounging in a chair? As a general rule, there needs to be some kind of illumination next to seating for these particular needs. If you favor a sofa, which cushion will you choose—the center or one of the ends? And will you be playing cards? Board games? Watching TV? Each of these activities will demand its own type of light, especially TV viewing.

A pet peeve of mine is seeing a TV placed above a mantel. To me, that looks extremely awkward and is usually much too high for comfortable viewing. On the other hand, you won't want to position the TV in a spot where your recessed lighting is beaming directly on it, although a modest amount of light in an otherwise darkened setting would be best for your eyes and reduce overall fatigue. Similarly, a great many movie houses are primed not to dim their lights to total darkness, but to allow a faint glow to remain visible. This lessens the harsh contrast between the bright screen and the dark auditorium, so audiences are never in total darkness.

Family rooms usually include a large sofa or some kind of seating arrangement in the center of the room—or, if not, on one of the walls. The sofa could be floating or centered in front of the fireplace, if there is one. My point is that no seating should necessarily be restricted to a wall with access to a power outlet. In a Park Avenue penthouse, we laid a custom-made rug, then positioned our furnishings on top of it, mainly a sofa with a lit table behind it. The table's surface was illuminated by LED light engines (see the glossary). We felt that the only way to light that setting appropriately would be to install a power strip right in the floor. This meant we would have to make a cut in that custom rug. How else to deliver task light to the center of a room decorated with an area rug?

I let my client decide if we could slice into that expensive floor covering. She listened carefully to what I described, and was okay with it, finally. So we installed a power outlet in the floor, directly below where the sofa table would sit, then placed two lamps on the table that supply light to the center of the room. My client was a savvy woman who understood lighting challenges and appreciated what well-conceived lighting could do for an interior and for anyone who would be using that room.

Charles Pavarini III inspects RGB light engines before the sofa-back table's translucent onyx top is lit. Such light engines produce an uninterrupted glow and enable it to change colors to alter the mood of a room. *Photograph: J. Randall Tarasuk*

Another task-lighting issue habitually involves a piano, which often finds its way into a family room. Whether it's an upright, a spinet, or a grand piano, it needs to be lit properly for playing and reading music. (For details on lighting pianos, see chapter 4, "The Flexible but Functional Dining Room").

The Library Look

A family room is a likely place to provide shelving for books, collections, and decorative accessories. This calls for decorative lighting, and in the past that challenge was not easily met. People would often install puck lights, directing their beams downward from the top shelf, but the beams would never quite reach the bottom. Today, however, with LED strip lighting tucked into notched-out corners of each tall stile, it's possible to light even the tallest shelf unit, from the crown all the way down to the base. (For detailed shelf-lighting tips, see page 38 and diagram on page 39.)

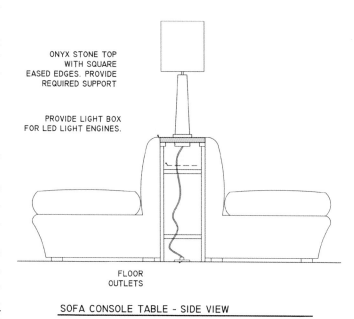

ONYX STONE TOP WITH SQUARE EASED EDGES. PROVIDE REQUIRED SUPPORT

PROVIDE LIGHT BOX FOR LED LIGHT ENGINES.

FLOOR OUTLETS

SOFA CONSOLE TABLE - SIDE VIEW

Integrated LED light engines illuminate the onyx top of a sofa-back table. The table lamp's power cord passes down through the table to an electrical outlet installed in the floor.

Plant Drama

Giving a plant the focus it deserves requires some kind of decorative lighting. Lit properly, a large plant or tree can be a marvelous natural addition to a room's decorating scheme, bringing a touch of outdoor life into the space. In my own room designs, I have often treated plants as sculptural objects that become particularly beautiful when lit from below.

How to light an indoor plant. If you don't do it by means of an up-light placed right in the container, you could do it by hanging a light fixture or adding a can light on one side of that container and directing the beam upward, into the plant. I think up-lighting can be dramatic, as though you're pulling light from another plane. When using fixtures on spikes sunk into the soil, I like to point light directly into the plantings, grazing the undersides of the leaves, where it creates playful shadows. Each fixture will act like a well light to illuminate the base of the plant or tree and then its trunk and branches. Light can also project beautiful leaf and branch shadows directly onto the ceiling and nearby walls.

Even in an informal family room, well-thought-out lighting makes a notable difference. It will not only enhance your overall room design and comfort but also add to the well-being of those using the space. Note that it's important to choose high-quality fixtures; they will look better, last longer, and project a clearer light.

Here is what you'll want to know when shopping for fixtures:
- Are the metals sturdy, not lightweight?
- Are the sockets high-quality porcelain, not plastic?
- Will a shade conceal the lightbulbs entirely?
- Do joints and other connections look solid?
- Will parts screw together easily?

Family Room Tips

- Know who will use this space, and how. Is there a need for additional levels of light, for reading, game playing, TV viewing, or providing higher lighting levels for anyone visually impaired?
- Use a minimum of 800 lumens (lm) around reading and work areas, 1,500 to 3,000 lm for the ambient lighting.
- To balance the room light, install fixtures throughout with the same light temperature in degrees kelvin (K).
- Make sure that the lighting controls can adjust to changing and special lighting requirements and can be preprogrammed to accommodate particular functions within the room (for details, see chapter 11, "True Tech").
- Because a family room is likely to get both daytime and nighttime use, include the availability of natural light in your plan.
- Use interesting portable floor lamps rather than immovable recessed fixtures to illuminate the room's dark corners.
- Make a design statement with your choice of fixtures, sconces, and other visible lighting implements.
- For an ultramodern alternative to a traditional table-style reading lamp, choose a stylish adjustable desk lamp.
- Avoid recessed lighting, which produces dark shadows. Instead, choose fixtures that will bounce light off the ceiling, thus simulating ambient illumination.
- Always think of a ceiling as an important source of reflected light.

A luxury interior designed with lighting that becomes the architecture of the room. *Design by Juan Montoya*

Layered lighting in a bedroom includes ambient light from two ceiling lanterns, a standing lamp, and a pendant over the night-stand paired with a gooseneck for ambience and reading in bed. Design by Pavarini Design, Inc. *Photographer: Phillip Ennis*

Getting the Bedroom Right

Light can be sensual; it can be comforting; it can even be dangerous. It goes beyond science or nature, or even art—it is as potent as life itself.
    —Ingo Maurer, designer of avant-garde light fixtures

Not only do we spend a third of our lives in bed, we are also likely to spend even more time in our bedrooms. We go there not only to sleep but also to read, study, watch TV, and sometimes work. We also select our clothes and get dressed there. All of this confirms that the bedroom is another space that has become truly multifunctional. It's also the most intimate space in our homes. Here, people are truly the focus, and peace and relaxation are paramount. Of all the rooms in your home, your bedroom may be the only one you live in when it's completely dark, completely bright, or somewhere in between.

There are multiple ways to light this space, and it is the room where all four aspects of home lighting come into play: ambient, task, decorative, and accent lighting, all of which were covered in chapter 1. Though all have equally important if often-subtle roles to play, flexibility and control should be the major concerns.

Having access to dimmers is an important component of lighting a bedroom, particularly a primary bedroom. There, lighting becomes a significant aspect of the room's overall style. For me, the key to good lighting design in any bedroom is creating flexibility, mainly through controlling light levels. When we talk about romantic lighting, for example, it doesn't necessarily mean where you place the light, but how you control it.

Establishing Focus

Because a bedroom is primarily for sleeping, bed placement must be the major design element and the primary focus of any lighting plan. Consider a bed the slumber zone, which must be consciously lit to support its function. Working on spec and without such a plan, builders and architects tend to install recessed ceiling lights in each corner of the room, so that no corner is in shadow or darkness.

By doing this, they can make the room look and feel larger—but only when empty. When furnished, a bedroom lit this way is certain to lack emphasis and focus. My approach is usually to install cove lighting or a center fixture. Each will graze a ceiling with light and compel your eye to move around the room.

A tray ceiling with LED cove lights can provide ambient lighting to suit every mood in a primary bedroom.

Layered lighting accentuates the texture of materials, and the RGB color-changing soffit lighting lends a romantic mood. Design by Pavarini Design, Inc. *Photographer: Dan Eifert*

A common mistake is lighting a bedroom with mainly overhead fixtures. Recessed lights are not recommended here because they flatten whatever texture and dimension you're trying to create. Bedroom lighting should not be even, or it will feel flat and bland. You want to encourage the eye to travel easily throughout the space. As with any room, my colleagues and I always begin our work with a floor plan and then, if it's new construction, indicate where we want electrical outlets and electrical boxes for decorative fixtures installed, or, if it's existing construction, pinpoint the location of existing electrical connections. That way, we can be sure of what we have to work with; we know our plan will not be effective unless there are electrical connections that support the placement of all lighting fixtures.

In new construction, you'll want a light switch installed just inside the bedroom door, so lights can be switched on or off when you enter or leave. You'll also want controls placed conveniently near the bed, preferably with three-way switches so you don't have to get out of bed to turn lights on and off.

My colleagues and I favor natural materials. White colors and shiny metals such as polished chrome or stainless steel can give bedrooms a cold and austere edge. We prefer materials such as stone, alabaster, wood, metals with a soft patina, and especially silks and linens. Silk, in particular, is known for its ability to transmit light. That's why a vast percentage of lampshades are made or lined with silk (see chapter 2, "Lampshade Lore").

Design-Defining Light

In a bedroom, as in any other room, light fixtures clearly express the design language. Pendants, floor lamps, table lamps, sconces—whatever we choose will impact the room's decorative style. When we talk about design, in visual terms we're speaking a specific language, one that embraces lighting, whether it's harsh, soft, disturbing, or soothing. Table lamps are effective, as are torchieres and standing lamps, as long as the light is diffused properly.

Symmetry is not always necessary in a bedroom, but even if your lighting design is asymmetrical, it will need to be balanced. For example, if you place a standing lamp on one side of the room, use a table lamp or another light source on the other. If you choose a sconce, it should be balanced by a table lamp—or perhaps another sconce—which will, in effect, make the arrangement appear symmetrical. Symmetry is achieved by the light in some form—not necessarily its fixture, but the decorative element that shapes its distribution.

If a primary bedroom includes a desk, club chair, or chaise, these furnishings should be supported by some type of task lighting. Layering the light eliminates significant highs and lows. Yes, you might want to give special attention to a work of art, but your primary goal should be to light the room so that people using it feel flattered by the light and can relax or perform tasks there. Overall, what's important is the ability to control light levels, because that's how you vary the mood. Soft music and an intoxicating scent may suggest an aura of romance, but lighting is what will define a mood more fully than other aspects of room design.

Another factor in bedroom design is the need to block light from streetlamps, neighbors' porches, or the early-morning sunrise. This is done with the creative use of window treatments such as valances, curtains, shades, and blinds. We sometimes place LED strip lights in the window in front of a shade or blind (or even behind a valance), so that in the evening a pale wash of light is visible between the window treatment and the shade behind it. In a bedroom we designed for a home in Tenafly, New Jersey, we installed subtle LED strip lights between the curtains and the shade, which lent a romantic ambient glow.

When choosing fabrics for lampshades, we'll specify ivory, off-white, or super-soft-white coverings so that when the light is off, the off-white tone is prominent. Then we'll line those shades in soft pink silk, so that when the light is on, it emits a flesh-tone wash that is highly flattering.

There is a history behind giving bedroom lighting a subtle tint. It was First Lady Jacqueline Kennedy who popularized pink lighting. When she traveled, her entourage always carried a stash of pink-toned light-bulbs. No matter where she was staying, one of the first things her staffers did was to replace the room's existing bulbs with the pink bulbs. These were known in the trade as "Jackie Kennedy Pink Bulbs."

Cove and Dome Lighting

Cove lighting with LEDs is an effective way to create unobtrusive ambient lighting. What it does is throw light onto the ceiling, so it can bounce back down into the room. This is not only ambient lighting but also mood lighting—romantic, to be sure—because a primary bedroom is a potentially intimate space where you'll want to create controllable mood lighting with absolutely no glare.

LED tape lighting is produced on a flexible, peel-and-stick substrate that can easily be wound on a reel, cut in specific places, and affixed to almost any surface. Specifications vary by manufacturer; however, there is virtually no limit to the color selections it can offer.

Another option, if permitted by the architecture, would be to install tiny LED strip lights around the perimeter of an oculus, a round ceiling dome. This great architectural feature is shaped to bounce light back into a space. Obviously, building an oculus can be done only in a tall room with a tray ceiling on a top floor, or in a room with attic or plenum space above the ceiling line. Either way, sensitive design and detailed construction work is required. This also pertains to tray ceilings.

Dome lighting is a variation on cove lighting, because the LEDs that extend around the base of the dome will fill that space with an even wash of light. Then, because of that curved shape, light will be projected up, into the center of the dome, and then back down, into the room. This type of lighting, from above, seems to lift the ceiling plane, creating the illusion it is higher than it is. Note that a ray of light cannot be bent; it illuminates in a straight line from point A to point B.

Obviously, crafting a dome involves major construction and a desire to express a dramatic use of space. We did this in a bedroom on the second floor of a Long Island home, where it was possible to pierce the ceiling. The result of such costly construction was elegant indirect lighting and a striking design. Lighting a tray or vaulted ceiling involves many of the same issues. Whatever the outline, light reflected onto a shaped ceiling produces an effect that's as visually appealing as it is functional.

Reading in Bed

A swing-arm lamp enables you to read in bed without disturbing a partner who may wish to sleep. This wall-mounted fixture is strictly a task light; how well it performs will depend on how and where it's mounted. Standard procedure would be to position the center of the fixture 44 inches above a finished floor. That height can be arbitrary and might not suit everyone. If a very tall person is involved, ask him or her to assume a position that would be comfortable for reading in bed. Make sure that person is in a relaxed or slouched position; someone reading in bed would not likely sit tall. And note that the light should be focused on the reading surface.

There are other circumstances to consider when positioning bedside swing-arm lamps: A book, magazine, or newspaper is usually held at shoulder height, so the wall lamp should be installed at a height between the reader's head and shoulders.

In another calculation, the bottom of the shade should be slightly below eye level. At that height, you can feel confident that the light will project properly on whatever is being read. In bedrooms expansive enough to include commodious nightstands, we'll often opt for a pair of table lamps topped with translucent shades. When space is tight and nightstand space is minimal, we'll hang ceiling pendants, one on each side of the bed. For a more contemporary look, we'll place multiple hanging fixtures at different heights. Their height differences give the space an artistic flair.

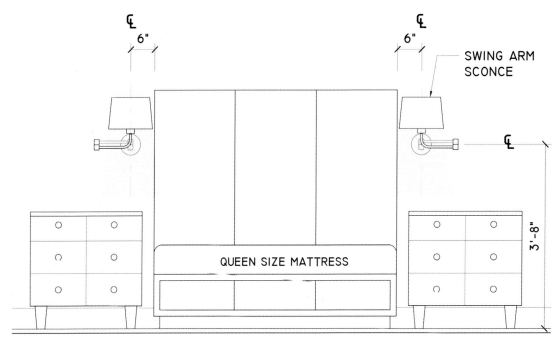

6"   6"

SWING ARM SCONCE

QUEEN SIZE MATTRESS

3'-8"

Standard dimensions for positioning bedside swing-arm lamps to allow for optimum reading in bed

One way to provide bedside lighting is to hang multiple pendant lights above a nightstand. Their staggered lengths add decorative interest and leave a clear surface on the nightstand. Design by Pavarini Design, Inc. *Photograph: Phillip Ennis*

What about a Kindle or iPAD, which has its own adjustable light? Sure, you can read in the dark on these devices, but the contrast between the lighted screen and room darkness will be harsh. It is less fatiguing to absorb the words on the screen when there's a slight wash of light around it.

If we have the ability to install a chandelier in a primary bedroom, chances are we won't center it. For maximum interest, we'll usually hang it directly over the foot of the bed or above a bench at the foot of the bed. That way, we won't be concerned about people bumping their heads. In a room with an 8-foot ceiling, finding an appropriate chandelier could be a challenge. You'll need one with no more than a 12-inch drop. Position a hanging fixture where it's unlikely that no one will be walking or standing under it—or choose a surface-mount fixture.

When working in a modern style, I opt for large-scale fixtures because of their impressive impact, though they must coordinate with the scale of the space. In a room with an 8-foot ceiling, for example, an oversized chandelier might be a prohibitive choice, but you could select a lamp with a slightly larger shade. Varying the size of the room's light fixtures can reinforce a modern concept and add to the room's visual interest.

Clearly, overhead lights would not produce an appropriate environment for bedtime reading, due to possible glare, but a height-appropriate table lamp would certainly work. And if that lamp were wired to a dimmer, it would be possible to keep the light level low enough not to disturb someone sleeping, while still providing sufficient reading light. Keep in mind, though, that beams of light are not going to pour out unless the shade is translucent.

If the lampshade is opaque, the illumination will be directed down (possibly also up), rather than out to light your reading material. For optimum reading light in bed, I suggest using a gooseneck reading lamp in addition to a swing-arm or table lamp.

An adjustable gooseneck sconce supplies direct lighting for reading in bed. Design by Pavarini Design, Inc. *Photograph: Phillip Ennis*

The Wardrobe Challenge

When positioning light fixtures in a closet, remember that there is a minimum code-specified distance between a light fixture, stored clothing, and any combustible items. That's true whether it's a wall sconce or a ceiling fixture. Check local building codes to ensure that you're in compliance. And note that your best lighting choices are LEDs because they emit so little heat. Conversely, halogens are not recommended here because of their heat.

A closet is a place to store clothes, not a place to get dressed. Most people select what they want to wear and then take it into the bedroom. Even so, closet lighting is extremely important, because it allows you to affirm your preferences and make sure that all the items you select work well together.

If it's a typical closet, between 28 and 30 inches deep, we'll illuminate the interior by installing a linear LED fixture directly above the header over the door. We'll want to make sure the light intensity (lumens) and color rendition (CRI) are correct for the space. For us, the optimum is 2700K to 3000K and a color rendition index (CRI) of 95 or more.

For socially active clients, I like to provide two circuits in a closet, one at 2700K, say, the other at 3000K, to ensure proper lighting for daytime and evening. It is also wise to use tunable white bulbs, which allow you to change the color temperature (kelvin) to simulate daytime or evening lighting, so that you can choose clothes accordingly. Tunable white lighting can be adjusted from 2000K to 4000K.

A walk-in closet presents a different challenge—to install general overhead illumination plus more finite lighting. To further illuminate a wardrobe, you can obtain clothing rods with tiny LED lights recessed into the bottom of each rod, so that the clothes are lit by the rod that supports them– a trick that would have been impossible in earlier eras. A capacious luxury closet might also have a cabinet with drawers fitted out with two vertical LED strips, one on each side, that are activated when you open the doors.

This closet pole sends light downward so that clothing can be easily selected. *Photo courtesy of Häfele America Co.*

Häfele

To make everything visible in a custom-designed man's closet, overhead lighting pairs with a strip light on either side of glass-enclosed wardrobes. Design by Pavarini Design, Inc. *Photograph: J. Randall Tarasuk*

People usually get dressed in daylight and stand in front of a mirror to evaluate their choices. For full-length mirrors, make sure the fixtures project light outward toward the person standing at the mirror, not behind them or back toward the mirror.

If the ceiling is wood, drywall, or plaster, I install adjustable ceiling fixtures, positioned slightly in front of the mirror and angled toward the person so he or she is well lit. Typically these are recessed or track fixtures placed on both sides of the mirror, 12 to 15 inches from the surface and aimed into the room. They should be adjustable, so that the light washes over the person standing at the mirror.

If the ceiling is impenetrable, I install a light at the top center of each panel—whether it's a flat mirror or a trifold—or install each light directly on the face of the mirror, about 7 feet above the floor. We may have to cut into the mirror so we can position the accompanying junction box behind it.

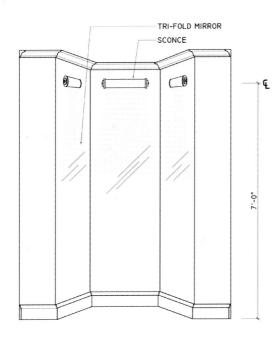

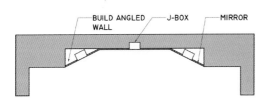

Mirrored panels with center-mounted sconces create an ideal dressing-room setting.

Guests' and Children's Rooms

A guest room calls for similar considerations, with less emphasis on creating a romantic aura. Lighting a children's bedroom is an entirely different challenge. In addition to sleeping, children read, get dressed, study at desks, and play games in their room. So flexibility should be a prime consideration. A desk needs to be well lit to keep the youngster alert and focused on what he or she is doing.

No matter what the challenge, keep in mind that proper illumination should point up design elements. Accent lights can draw the eye to various points of interest, taking you on a visual journey around the bedroom. Task lights provide not only utility but also the opportunity to light a design element on your bedroom desk or bedside table. And chandeliers provide dazzling romantic visual experiences by themselves, as well as through the light they emit.

Bedroom Lighting Tips

• A misconception of lighting this or any space is that you need to illuminate it fully. Instead, design so that you can incorporate multiple points of light.

• A bedroom deserves a feeling of intimacy. Use as few recessed fixtures as possible; they can create shadows and unflattering light.

• Lighting an average bedroom requires 1,500 to 2,000 lumens (lm).

• Layer the light, and be mindful that a bedroom is a place for relaxation, which calls for a tranquil atmosphere.

• Using tunable white LED bulbs will enable you to create a desired mood by changing color while maintaining the desired brightness.

• Provide good reading lights at the bed, desk, and chair, and task lighting for dressing. For maximum flexibility, all bedroom lighting should be dimmer controlled.

• A swing-arm lamp (task light) is best for reading in bed. Mount it 44 inches above the floor and approximately 6 inches away from the side of the bed.

• Pair a reading light with one or more bedside lamps—either a lamp on the nightstand or a hanging fixture above it.

• Overhead light can be achieved with a cluster of pendants above a nightstand.

• Because a bedroom may also be used throughout the day, incorporate natural light into a lighting plan.

• In a child's bedroom, specify at least one whimsical fixture, perhaps used as a night light.

For a primary bedroom in Tribeca, in downtown Manhattan, we installed a trifold mirror in a recess in a closet. The mirror's two side panels could be adjusted for viewing your image from the front, side, or back. Because the ceiling was concrete—typical in New York's newer apartment buildings—we mounted wall sconces with frosted lenses near the top of the trifold mirror. We chose three fixtures, one to light the center of each mirrored panel, and made sure the light was directed outward so the person would be lit properly.

In a similar situation, instead of full-length mirrors you might hang a shorter mirror above a dresser or wardrobe. Here, a table lamp with a translucent shade would be appropriate. Again, make sure the lamp light is directed outward rather than toward the ceiling or floor.

In a child's bedroom, whimsical lighting can create a feeling of playfulness, warmth, and comfort for young ones. *Design by Martyn Lawrence Bullard*

Closet Lighting Tips

• Give your closet a sense of style by choosing a statement fixture plus lighting that will make you feel inspired.

• To conserve power, use motion sensors instead of switches.

• Flush-mount fixtures are a good choice. They emit diffused light that can bounce off the ceiling and create a bright environment.

• Augment closet lighting with a chandelier or pendant that adds personality and decorative flair.

• By simulating daytime and evening light, tunable white lights offer the best functionality for choosing outfits to be worn under different kinds of light and at different times of day.

• LED strip lighting is ideal for closets. Install it under cabinets, at the upper front of built-ins, or embedded in the sides of cabinetry.

• Large walk-in closets lend themselves to inspired choices such as sconces and decorative overhead fixtures. Make sure they provide sufficient light.

• As a fire-safety precaution, install recessed fixtures 6 inches away from clothing, whether shelved or hanging from rods. For surface-mounted fixtures, there must be at least 12 inches between each fixture and the items you're storing.

• Do not use bare bulbs. For fire safety, every lightbulb in a closet should be enclosed in a globe or other type of housing.

In a kitchen lit exclusively by LEDs, a linear light "ribbon" recessed in the ceiling traces the edge of the island and counter. Adding decorative flair to task and ambient lighting, an oversized pendant and back-wall sconces enrich the overall style. Design by Pavarini Design, Inc. *Photograph: Phillip Ennis*

Kitchens, Baths, and Then Some

One of the strongest characteristics of genius is the power of lighting its own fire.
—John Watson Foster, a former US secretary of state

Lighting decisions for the kitchen, laundry room, and bathroom are usually subordinated to a single significant concept: function. Although the tasks may be different, the lighting needs of these spaces are really quite similar.

As the epicenter of home life, the kitchen is both a workspace and a gathering spot. People tend to take this notion for granted nowadays, but it was not always so. Kitchens were once housed in structures set apart from living spaces, and when they were finally brought under one roof they were relegated to airless, light-challenged basements. No one went there except the person who prepared the meals, largely by the light of the open fire on which food was cooked. Kitchens were also usually smoky because there was little or no ventilation. Candles and lanterns augmented firelight until late in the nineteenth century, when the Edison discovery promised long-lasting, electric-powered illumination that, in tone, closely approximated sunlight.

But change was not immediate. Cities and towns had to be wired to make it possible to electrify factories, offices, stores, and homes. It was well into the twentieth century when homes lit by electricity became the norm, and it was only then that the kitchen began its gradual integration into the structure of family life.

Our earliest in-home kitchens were predictably primitive—and certainly not decorative. These were not welcoming spaces. In addition to a cooking element, the kitchen contained a worktable or two on which essentials were stacked and food preparation was done. It wasn't until the early twentieth century that an Indiana-based company decided the kitchen could be made more functional and less chaotic if storage was provided.

Because of its location, the firm was called Hoosier Manufacturing, and the product they marketed was similarly labeled. Based on the traditional baker's cabinet, the three-section Hoosier was ostensibly the first piece of furniture designed and built specifically for kitchens.

Light from candles and the fireplace creates a warm glow in this traditional eighteenth-century English kitchen.

Decorative OLED pendants illuminate an island, and ambient lighting is provided with a continuous ribbon of light that traces the kitchen perimeter. The layered scheme also includes recessed lighting over the work surface and a decorative pendant over the dining table.

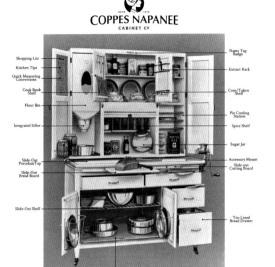

A late-nineteenth-century invention, the Hoosier was the first kitchen cabinet. It featured integrated storage compartments in addition to baking gadgetry and places to prepare food. *Photo courtesy of Coppes Napanee*

Measuring 4 by 6 feet, it was a compact unit whose shelves and drawers were fitted out to store sugar, flour, spices, and containers, and it also included a flat surface for rolling out and kneading dough. The unit's four thin legs rested on casters, so the unit could be moved where needed, and when discovered today—at yard sales and antiques fairs—Hoosier cabinets are likely to end up decorating family rooms and breakfast areas

in homes whose owners love its handsome vintage design. During the years when it was built and marketed—from 1899 until well into the 1920s—the all-in-one Hoosier was considered strictly utilitarian; no one would have thought to put it on display in a den or dining room. But it pioneered the development of the multipurpose kitchen cabinets that have come to resemble fine furniture in many homes today.

Since the mid-twentieth century, the kitchen has expanded markedly in size and scope. Soon after World War II, the kitchen's fourth wall began disappearing, opening it up to an adjacent eating area, dining room, family room, or even the living room. Eventually, all signs of kitchen functionality were being downplayed or concealed. What was once a showcase for cookware, glassware, flatware, herbs, and spices became closed cabinetry, with bins for bread and vegetable storage, and so-called appliance garages for coffee makers, toasters, mixers, blenders, and microwaves. Homemakers began favoring clean looks, and designers responded. They also came through when it was clear that a single light in the center of the space could never fulfill all the demands of what, for a lighting designer, has become a predictable challenge.

The kitchen triangle still prevails. The basic sink-stove-refrigerator configuration, often referred to as the "golden triangle," is still the most predictable traffic pattern in any kitchen, large or small, compact or expanded. It continues to reflect the room's basic functions—preparing, serving, and storing food. That triangle has often been extended or expanded, and in some kitchens there is more than one triangle.

Lit and balanced for dining and cooking, a modern kitchen is illuminated by cove lighting, pendants, and under-cabinet LED strip lighting.

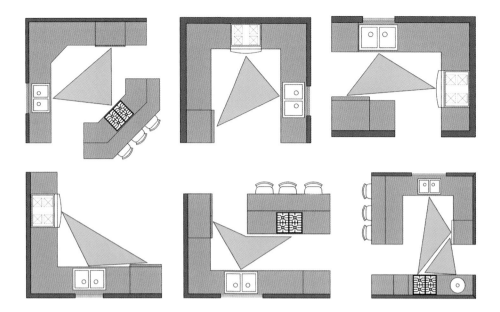

Six different layouts highlight the "golden triangle" of modern kitchen design: meal preparation, cooking, and food storage.

Kitchen designers typically focus on step-saving when determining where to place the room's primary elements. After these units have been positioned, you'll want to determine how many people will use the space at one time. Where will people stand to rinse, cut, and chop fresh vegetables; load and unload the dishwasher; fill plates and serve the food. Then consider how to illuminate each work zone for the number of cooks involved, so that lighting throughout the room is even, since all the functions add up to the kitchen's overall purpose. In other words, you not only need to light individual work areas but to link them so there is no dip in lighting.

That can be more challenging than it seems. A recent Manhattan apartment kitchen we designed had 8-foot concrete ceilings, so it was impossible to channel into them or move the electrical boxes. The solution to providing overhead lighting in the work zones was to install a shallow fixture measuring 10 feet long by 2 feet wide by ⅝ inch deep, with integrated strip LEDs.

The fixture is equipped with flanges that allow it to be plastered right into a concrete or Sheetrock ceiling. Yes, the entire replastered ceiling ended up being ⅜ inch lower than before, but the change is almost imperceptible, and the result is an unbroken ribbon light level with the ceiling—a seamless integration.

These LED ribbons provide an opportunity to create a variety of original designs. We can extend a light strip across the ceiling and butt it up to a wall or even extend it down the wall. An alternative would be to drop the ceiling at least 2 inches so an electrical box could be installed for a chandelier, hanging pendant, or surface-mounted fixture.

Under-counter lighting has been around for a while, usually comprising halogen or sometimes xenon fixtures. But LED strips are eminently more practical, and thus more desirable, since they can easily be tucked into tight spaces beneath wall cabinets, lighting the countertop. Interior cabinet lighting is supplied by

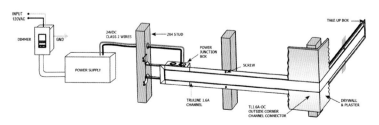

Installed within walls and ceilings, a plaster-in LED lighting system is integrated into ⅝-inch Sheetrock, supplying uninterrupted linear illumination without reducing ceiling height. *Diagram courtesy of PureEdge Lighting*

Pure-EDGE LIGHTING

In a modern kitchen, LED systems and LED plaster-in recessed lighting are flush-mounted within Sheetrock, providing illumination without apertures or trim. *Photo courtesy of PureEdge Lighting*

many manufacturers, but any cabinet that lacks inside lighting will have to be illuminated. When a cabinet door is opened, it should be possible to see all the way into the space.

If you're dealing with an impenetrable ceiling, you will have to decide how you can shine light so you can see into each storage space. Also, if the ceiling itself is low, a hanging fixture could get in the way of a swinging cabinet door. That's why we tend to opt for ribbons of light, which are clean, barely noticeable when installed, and unencumbered by any kind of fixture.

Indeed, kitchen design seems to be moving away from visible light fixtures. The look is getting more modern and much, much cleaner. Recent years have seen more and more kitchen cabinetry made to resemble furniture styles; thus a kitchen may have cabinets resembling the furniture in other parts of a home. Although kitchen lighting doesn't have to define an owner's decorating style, it should reinforce the feel and function you hope to achieve.

Whenever I use any type of recessed ceiling fixture—halogen, LED, or even incandescent—its placement in a kitchen is critical. Knowing where to hang lights means that no one will ever need to perform a task in darkness. I can't imagine anything worse than having to work at a counter with the light behind you, putting whatever you're doing in shadow. My rule of thumb is to install the light source so that its center is directly above the leading edge of the kitchen counter.

When lighting an island, I try to illuminate the whole thing rather than creating pools of light. Particularly if the island has two sides—one for kitchen prep, the

other for informal dining—I would place an overhead light source near the center so the surface is evenly lit. You're not designing decoratively or dramatically here. Functionality comes first; decorative touches follow.

In a kitchen, you're basically lighting the surfaces, even if it's the place where grocery bags are unloaded or packaged foods are stacked in the freezer. Your goal should be to light those surfaces so you can see without strain. When a kitchen is adequately lit, you may not be actually aware of it. Rather, you'll probably start to feel that something is wrong if you can't see well enough. Sight is as critical to our understanding of a space as the functions within it, so it definitely needs to be considered.

In a traditional kitchen, surface-mount fixtures and pendants provide ambient lighting throughout. They can be lamped with LED-retrofit bulbs at 3000K. Design by Martyn Lawrence Bullard.

In a home crafts room, a recessed ribbon of light washes a wall, an LED plaster-in system supplies continuous workstation light, and a trimless recessed LED fixture supplies ambient illumination. A wall sconce adds decorative style and additional ambient lighting to the design. Design by Pavarini Design, Inc. *Photograph: J. Randall Tarasuk*

In a transitional or traditional kitchen, I'm likely to use decorative light fixtures because they enhance the visual experience of entering or looking into the space, and also reinforce the style I have established. Pendants or a chandelier can be quite effective. They not only shed light directly on an important surface—an island, dining table, breakfast table, or work zone—but also lend visual impact. And I may mount one or more sconces in key locations to augment the impact of my overheads.

Depending on the size of your kitchen, you might also want to interrupt the ceiling plan with decorative fixtures. The light should either be directed downward or placed to add ambient lighting. This means the diffuser or lampshade should be translucent, so that the light is emitted sideways or in all outward directions—not just downward, which creates pools of light rather than overall illumination. A metal or dark-painted shade will focus light in just one direction. But if that shade is made of fabric, glass, or even plastic, your fixture will be projecting light all around the room. That's another reason you need to know how a kitchen will be used—by whom, and the work zones within it—before completing the lighting plan.

Laundry Room Basics

Treat the laundry room primarily as task-oriented space. After all, it's where specific work is done: separating white clothes and colors, loading washers and dryers, folding and stacking. Most laundry room designs are pretty basic, but a small supply cabinet would be a useful addition. If there's enough space, a foldaway ironing board and a table for folding laundered items are nice to include.

This is clearly not a room that calls for decorative sconces or fussy chandeliers, so most of your essential task light will come from overheads. That said, high-quality lighting is important here. You'll want to be sure to have great color rendition (a high CRI of 90 plus) and that the light temperature is appropriate for experiencing color (3000K). As with a closet, where I might be matching a tie to a suit jacket, a laundry room needs to be lit well enough to separate blue socks from black or dark brown. But there's no reason to approach the laundry room with the sensitivity required when dealing with other spaces. After completing your laundry chores, you're likely to turn off the lights, close the door behind you, and move on.

There are always exceptions! I once visited a showhouse laundry room designed as an inviting place to linger. It included a swivel chair and desk, a lamp, and a TV and music system. Frankly, I think a laundry room, which is not heavily trafficked, would be a better place for a desk than a kitchen, which in many households has become a kind of public space. For a showhouse, the sky's the limit, of course—whatever amenity there's room for will be included. But normally, a laundry room is not a space you'd leave open, with lights on, for a visual experience.

Balanced lighting creates glare-free functionality in a laundry room. Design by Bonnie J. Steves Interior Design. *Photo by Nick Johnson Photography*

Beauty in the Bath

When lighting a kitchen, you're focused on surfaces where specific tasks are performed. In a bathroom, you're mainly lighting the person using the space. As a place for brushing your teeth, combing your hair, applying or removing makeup, and dealing with bodily functions, it's an intimate space that should reflect how you feel about yourself. The focus should not be the task but on how you see yourself after it is done. Thus, mirrors should be placed so you can see yourself *and* your surroundings.

Overhead vanity lighting is generally poor, at best, because it creates shadows under your eyes, no matter how old you are. These shadows make it difficult to perform grooming needs effectively. Developers often install a light directly above the center of a sink. Well, that might light your head and nose pretty well, but it's not going to light your face in a flattering way.

If I have to rely on recessed overhead lights and am unable to install eye-level sconces, I will produce cross-lights by installing an adjustable recessed ceiling fixture on each side of the sink. The light should have some beam spread so it works for people of varying heights. You won't want to focus that light directly on the sink, because the sink itself doesn't have to be lit. You'll want to light the face.

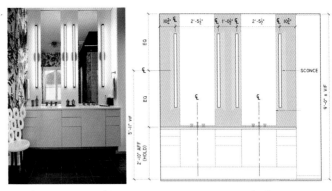

Careful placement of linear LED sconces in a primary bathroom ensures flattering vanity lighting. Design by Pavarini Design, Inc. *Photograph: Phillip Ennis*

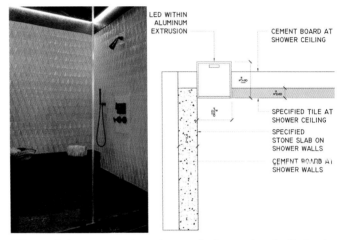

LED cove lighting around the perimeter of a shower gives the illusion the ceiling is floating. Design by Pavarini Design, Inc. *Photograph: Phillip Ennis*

Taking a cue from theater-lighting designers, place overhead lights at a 45-degree angle from their subject. At that angle, your whole face can be lit perfectly. When such an arrangement is not possible, I'll place one light overhead, a few inches out from the wall mirror, and angle it downward, toward my face. I'll augment this light with sconces on either side of the mirror, so I get light on each plane of my face as well as overhead. Mainly, as in the kitchen, I want to establish even light. When you are standing at the far end of a bathroom and catch a glimpse of yourself in the mirror, you don't want to be half in light, half in shadow.

I like clean ceiling planes in any room, but especially in a bathroom. While light should be positioned directly over the water closet, I usually brighten that area with sconces. Similarly, in a shower, I want the light to be truly functional. In the primary bath of a house in Oceanport, New Jersey, we covered the entire shower stall in iridescent glass tile. LED lights tucked into the ceiling fully washed those iridescent tile walls—we used no overheads. The lighting was subtle but effective; you couldn't tell where the light was coming from.

The ceiling of that bathroom was clear except for a single decorative fixture, which we placed to project some overall lighting into the room. Its form and style reinforced the overall effect we wanted to achieve. However, most of the lighting came from the walls, not the ceiling.

Often, bathroom lighting is projected from the mirror itself. The mercury on the back has been eliminated, the back of the mirror has been frosted, and LEDs have been installed there. In this way the mirror becomes part of the lighting plan.

A round mirror with integrated LED lighting adds a touch of drama in a powder room. Design by Pavarini Design, Inc. *Photograph: © Marco Ricca Studio*

Powder Room Glamour

Powder rooms, used mostly by guests, typically have only two functions. A simple light plan will do: two sconces or one overhead fixture, or both. With all three, you'd also want dimmers to adjust the light levels. You want to create an ambience that's soft, flattering, glamorous, and maybe even a little sexy.

I once used the powder room in a home I was visiting and was surprised to see that the major light source came from behind a big mirror over the sink. When I tried using that mirror, I found I couldn't see myself. Yes, with its halo of light, I could see the sink and the counter easily. But there was no way to direct light onto the person standing there. You can certainly install a mirror that emits its own lovely glow, but you may need to augment it with other forms of lighting.

Mirrors aside, I think the best way to infuse a powder room with drama is through the use of light. Perhaps that comes from my background in theater. My take is that you can have beautiful colors, forms, and styles—in a powder room or any other space—but what really makes a room sing is how it's perceived. And what will invariably shape that perception is light—the type of light you choose and the way it's positioned and presented.

Lighting Tips for the Kitchen, Bathroom, and Closet

Kitchen

• Spread out the lumens. Don't use only a few fixtures with high lumens. Use a combination of accent, ambient, and task lighting elements that can be controlled individually.

• Install LED strip lighting in the toe kick of your cabinets. It will provide another layer of ambient lighting and is an easy way to give cabinets an updated look.

• To make sure your countertop work areas are well lit, consider under-cabinet illumination. I prefer installing LED strips near the front edge of the wall cabinets' bottom surface. Lights placed near the back will focus light mainly on the backsplash.

• Puck lights focus pools of light on a work surface and backsplash.

• To determine proper spacing between recessed (ambient) lights, divide the room-height measurement by 2. For an 8-foot ceiling, for example, the fixtures should be 4 feet apart; 5 feet apart for a 10-foot ceiling. This rule can be broken, depending on the lumens, the type of light, and its purpose (ambient, accent, or task).

• My preference is to overlight a room, but use dimmable bulbs to control the brightness.

• Your kitchen's wow factor can be the light fixtures. Choose fixtures that enhance the space, reinforce your aesthetic, and deliver great-quality light.

• Some kitchen tasks need bright light, others less so. Adding a separate dimmer for each fixture or group of fixtures adds great flexibility.

• Linear suspension lights work well over islands. Install them no lower than 40 inches above the countertop (measured from the bottom of the fixture).

• If you light drawer interiors, you'll always be aware of their contents—a great convenience, particularly if the lights can be made to snap on and off when the drawers are opened and closed.

• Install a task light directly over the middle of your sink. Whether it's recessed, flush mounted, or on a pendant, make sure that light is on its own circuit.

A modern kitchen functions perfectly without conventional recessed lights, thanks to layered indirect lighting mounted in the coffered ceiling and within the cabinetry. Floating glass cabinets form a dramatic centerpiece with a thrilling mix of Smallbone hand craftsmanship complemented by state-of-the-art technology. *Photo of the Icarus Kitchen by Smallbone*

• When remodeling, consider stylish new fixtures—they are among the best ways to update a kitchen.

Bathroom

• Mount sconces a few inches to the left and right of a mirror centered above a vanity.

• The backplate of any vertical fixture should be installed at eye level.

• The shade opening of a sconce downlight needs to be below eye level to avoid glare.

• Conversely, the shade opening of a sconce uplight must be slightly above eye level, so you don't see the light source when you look into the fixture.

• If considering pendant lights in lieu of sconces, make sure the light source is at eye level, to give your vanity an elevated feeling and an atypical look.

• If you prefer an adjustable recessed light, place it so light is directed over the center of the sink, and angle it to light the center of your face—choose an angle that doesn't put any aspect of your face in shadow.

• Adding toe-kick lighting under the vanity is another way to add light to the space—and is also good as a night light.

• If hanging a fixture above a tub, be mindful of your local electrical code. To make sure no bather can touch the fixture while standing in water, that fixture should not hang lower than 7½ feet above the high-water line.

• Choose fixtures with similar finishes to maintain design continuity.

• Over-mirror fixtures are adequate but not ideal; light from above can create shadows on your face.

• Keep in mind that there are LED fixtures and vanity mirrors with warm-dim capabilities, allowing you to adjust the light between 2200K and 5000K.

Closet

• Light it with LEDs; they're energy efficient and long lasting and emit minimal heat.

• Being able to control the light temperature, which should be 2700K to 3000K, will enable you to make good color choices, and keep in mind that the higher the CRI (color-rendering index), the more accurate the portrayal of color in your home.

• Install LED strip lights at the base of closet cabinets. They will provide additional glow and give the closet a modern look.

• Because LED bulbs come in a range of lumens, they can achieve various visual effects, depending on cabinetry color and existing ambient or natural light.

• Use dimmers for additional customization.

• A small, 30-to-80-square-foot closet is best illuminated with 500 to 1,000 lumens.

• If an electrical connection is unavailable, consider wireless closet lights. Battery operated, they are extremely reliable. Many have energy-efficient motion sensors, eliminating the need for a switch.

• If installing lights means using a remote driver, make sure it's positioned away from anything combustible—an upper shelf would be ideal.

• A closet with a window is a luxury. Keep it free of light-blocking clutter and choose light, airy window treatments if needed.

Pierced-metal sconces filter decorative lighting and up-and-down illumination along a hall. Ambient lighting is directed down from recessed ceiling fixtures. Design by Claudia Leccacorvi. *Photograph: Brando Barré*

Transitional Spaces

Light belongs to the heart and spirit. Light attracts people, it shows the way, and when we see it in the distance, we follow it.
    —Ricardo Legorreta, architect

Lighting the Hallway

A hallway signals a transition, an area of passage. Regardless of its dimensions, it leads you from one part of a home to another, sometimes to the exterior. In lighting a hall, my goal is not only to make the space inviting but also to create enough interest to motivate you to move through that space. A lot of homeowners use hallways as galleries; their walls become surfaces for displaying art, whether it is paintings, engravings or prints, children's drawings, or family photos. The design goal here is to create a warm, safe environment in which to navigate a home.

Most hallways lack even one window, so attention must be paid to how they are lit. Even with skylights, or one or more windows, we're still faced with a nighttime challenge to counter the darkness. If a hallway has windows, I would light them at night by installing an LED strip above each one, with an apron to shield the direct light and eliminate glare.

Dynamic light fixtures augmented by recessed lights elevate an otherwise simple entrance foyer. Design by Bennett Leifer. *Photograph: © Marco Ricca Studio*

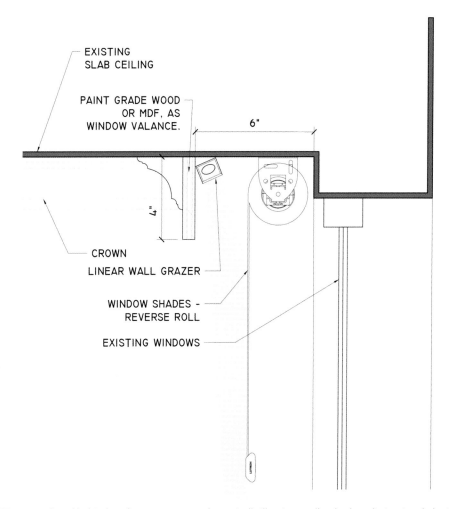

EXISTING
SLAB CEILING

PAINT GRADE WOOD
OR MDF, AS
WINDOW VALANCE.

6"

4"

CROWN
LINEAR WALL GRAZER

WINDOW SHADES -
REVERSE ROLL

EXISTING WINDOWS

An LED strip is placed behind a valance or apron to dramatically illuminate roller shades, eliminating dark windows at night.

A combination like the one shown in the diagram above can illuminate any type of shade or drapery panel and make sure there won't be any dark punctuation in the space. My team and I specify LEDs primarily because of their low-energy consumption and also because of their low heat emission. That makes it possible to place them right next to fabrics, without the flammability concerns that exist with halogen or incandescents.

A repetition of fixtures. I sometimes stagger sconces from one side of a hall to the other—to bounce light back and forth throughout the passageway. I always repeat the same style of fixture, whether it's a pendant or a surface mount, its size dependent on ceiling height. Pendants, more appropriate where the ceiling is high, don't simply project light straight down but also bathe the walls with light. What about recessed fixtures? They have their place, but I don't like using them in hallways because they project pools of light downward and create shadows.

On Track for Art

To illuminate a hallway that acts as an art gallery, consider installing a monorail, a track that's ceiling mounted or embedded into the ceiling for a more integrated, minimalist appearance. Depending on what you're lighting, try varying the type of fixtures hung from the rail. This type of lighting offers great flexibility when moving pieces of art. This form of accent lighting both optimizes the visibility of each piece and draws the eye from one piece to the next.

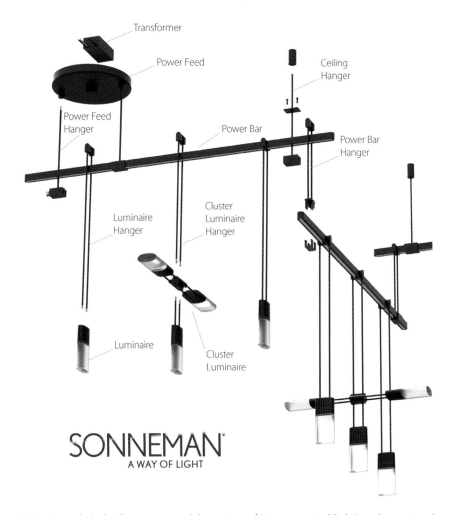

SONNEMAN®
A WAY OF LIGHT

Delicately scaled, the Sonneman modular system of interconnected lighting elements and suspended LEDs integrates decorative and functional luminaires harmoniously. Sonneman suspenders offer the capability of adding either focused light or the soft glow of indirect illumination to any application. *Photo courtesy of Sonneman—a Way of Light*

In effect, your eye will pull you as you move down the hall. Here, as in any defined space, light will direct you to look at different aspects of the space. An even distribution of light would make a hallway feel institutional. On the other hand, when light fixtures are so spread out that dark patches appear between them, your line of vision is interrupted. That's why, however, there should be highs and lows—subtle shifts rather than dramatic ones. You can create undulating light down a hallway, but you won't want blazing bright light or light so dim that shadows or dark patches are created. And you don't ever want to mix the two.

Cove lighting can be an effective way to light a hallway. This would necessitate tucking a fixture behind crown molding and also require the crown to drop a bit

SONNEMAN

from the ceiling so that light can be emitted—ideal if the ceiling is barrel vaulted. If the ceiling is flat, the crown must be dropped 6 to 8 inches, far enough so that light hitting the ceiling will also bounce down to the floor. But even if cove lighting seems the best way to illuminate a particular hallway, I'd recommend adding sconces to ensure the entire path is lit, not just the ceiling plane.

The recessed ceiling above the sculpture contains hidden lighting that illuminates the art piece from above. Flush-mount fixtures down the hallway direct the eye to the sculpture. *Photo courtesy of Cerno*

What about Furniture?

If the hallway is wide, you could include some furnishings—for example, a chair or a long bench with or without a back. If there is room for a table or a console, include a decorative lamp or two. Lamps with shades always add a warm feeling. Of course, the hall must provide an uncluttered pathway that's safe and easy to navigate.

If a hallway ends at a wall—with no door leading elsewhere—you could place a piece of art or sculpture there, to draw the eye to the end of the space.

The object you choose will need to be lit appropriately and also have the potential to create drama—another effective way to capture people's attention and, in a sense, draw them through the space. Here, installing a recessed fixture would be the best way to give it emphasis. If you're dealing with artwork, picture lights would also be appropriate.

Of course, some hallways have a turn, an intersection linking two corridors, and often that intersection is marked by a vaulted ceiling. This is a good place to hang a decorative pendant. It makes clear, to anyone looking down either hallway, that another path lies ahead.

Architectural Opportunities

If a hall is large and has architectural elements—arches, columns, pilasters, panels, or crowns—consider focusing light directly on these elements—another good way to pull you into the space and then down the hallway. Cove lighting works well and would require dropping the crown a few inches to make installation possible. Installing the crown with an inch and a half projection from the wall plane is particularly effective if the ceiling is barrel vaulted. Here, I would opt for LED strips so that light can be beamed all the way up to the ceiling, then bounced down to illuminate the floor plane.

Or, you could light the walls rather than the ceiling. To do this, position the crown about an inch and a half out from the wall plane, which will create a pocket for the light strips directly under the crown. The cavity should be at least an inch deep—more if you are using a diffuser lens on the LED strip. By all means, you'll want to diffuse the nodes so a continuous beam of light is created. And do make sure you see only the beam from below, not its source of light.

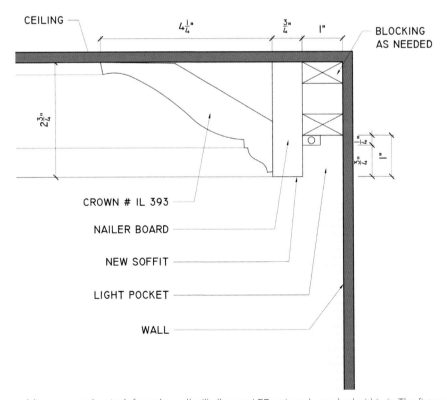

A crown molding mounted an inch from the wall will allow an LED strip to be tucked within it. The fixture will graze light downward, highlighting specialty wall treatments or wall coverings.

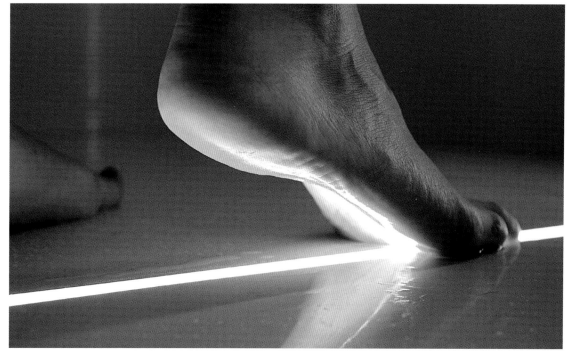

Diffusers cut glare from floor-installed strip lighting in a hallway. Manufacturers offer similar products for damp locations such as bathrooms and showers. *Photo courtesy of KLUS*

Another approach to lighting hallway architecture is possible if the project is still under construction. You can light the walls from bottom to top by embedding a ribbon of LED light into the floor on each side of the hall. Or you can install recessed cans into the floor, which, by up-lighting the walls, will emphasize the verticality of the space. However, you'll need to cover the entire installation with a sandblasted diffuser, preferably glass, to eliminate glare (you can light from below even when the ceiling is only 8 or 8½ feet high). In this case, however, the projected light beams will not only illuminate the walls but also focus light on the ceiling for a dramatic effect.

Lighting a hallway from below can be really tricky, because you need to get into the floor to install the wiring and fixtures. Obviously, this is best done while a project is under construction. If there's a basement, however, you could do the installation from below rather than tearing up sections of flooring. Whatever your approach, and whether the floor surface is stone, wood, concrete, or tile, the diffuser that softens the light must be level with the flooring to avoid a tripping hazard. And the lens, which could be glass or high-grade plastic, must be sturdy enough to be stepped on repeatedly over time.

If you install floor lighting no more than a few inches away from each wall, there is little danger of it being in anyone's way. When people negotiate a hallway, they tend to stick to the center, and lights placed close to the wall will also minimize glare. Note that floor lighting can create visual cues, another way to direct you through the space.

I think it feels more modern and adds a sense of drama to light from the floor up, rather than from the ceiling down. Lighting that comes from the floor is energizing and uplifting. In this case I would avoid carpeting, so the light isn't obscured.

Stair Basics

Good lighting on stairways can be decorative but is always essential. As you're moving from one level to another, shadows or dark patches could be perilous. You'll want even lighting, so each step can be seen clearly. And, for safety as well as convenience, you'll always need lighting controls. If you embed stair lighting in the wall, illuminating every other step will be more than adequate—the light hitting one step will also reach the one above it.

If you want a more dramatic effect, you could always install light under the treads to illuminate the risers. That would require a modest lip on each tread so the light source isn't visible and eliminate glare. Another elegant way to light stairs is to choose handrails with integrated LEDs, or to install electrified rails that are lit from within.

Here are ways to light stairways *(left to right, top to bottom)*: wall lights placed above every step and landing; an LED retrofit stair extrusion gives light to the tread and riser of a staircase; LED strip lighting installed under the lip of each tread; integrated LED strips within the handrail. *Photos courtesy of KLUS*

A Case for the Mudroom

There's no need to make a decorative splash with mudroom lighting. But since this is a potentially high-traffic area—where people enter the house from the garage, garden, or back porch, sometimes carrying packages—efficient, nonglare lighting is essential. One or more pendant lights are effective, especially if the fixture allows light to project in multiple directions.

I don't recommend just recessed lighting, because it would likely create shadows. Sconces are possible; how many would depend on a mudroom's width and length. Another consideration: A mudroom often has space for some kind of furnishings, perhaps a place to drop packages or sort the daily mail. This could be a shallow table or a small chest or console. Topping that piece with a decorative lamp will create another welcome light source, adding a layer of light.

Layered lighting in a classically designed entrance hall draws you into the space. Design by Robert A. M. Stern Architects.

A freestanding or built-in unit with open cubicles would be a positive addition to a mudroom, particularly in households where youngsters rush in and out with sports gear and outerwear that might otherwise get tossed in a tangle somewhere. Cubbyholes take the curse off the sorting and organizing chore, but only if they are properly lit. Installing fixtures in or near each opening should not be necessary; overhead lighting is sufficient.

Ideally, I think recessed lights should be installed 6 to 8 inches beyond the outer edge of a cubbyhole. This differs from the way you usually light kitchen workspaces, where recessed overhead fixtures direct light down to the edge of the countertop. Standing at a kitchen counter, you're leaning over, so you wouldn't want lighting that puts you in shadow. Reaching into a cubby, you won't be close enough to block light from above.

The Entry

The entry hall is the place where first impressions are made—where a home's decorating style is first indicated. A chandelier makes a strong statement in a double-height entry hall, but only if it relates to the style of furnishings throughout the house. In other words, entry hall lighting should provide clues to how the home interior feels.

In multifamily buildings, if an entry has a stairway to a second level, the upper area should be lit the same way as the one below it. Whatever can be seen from the entry hall should be lit the same way as the entry area itself. You definitely don't want anyone ascending a dark stairway or looking up toward an area where the lighting is poor. My inclination would be to install something decorative at the top of the stairs, a pair of sconces rather than recessed lighting. I would try to achieve an effect that draws you up the stairs. A series of wall sconces, placed at equal intervals, would work well and could also have a dramatic effect.

In homes that have a double-height entry, I'll make sure that an Aladdin Light Lift is available. This is a cable system that allows a chandelier to be lowered for cleaning and relamping, then lifted back into place. Controlled by a keyed light switch, it's safer and more practical than mounting a tall ladder to deal with a fixture.

As I've suggested, whatever a hallway's size or volume, layering your lighting can involve multiple types of illumination—fixtures installed in the floor, in the ceiling, even in both walls. And there could be strip lights, sconces, pendants, or picture lights—perhaps even a chandelier. If there is artwork or an important

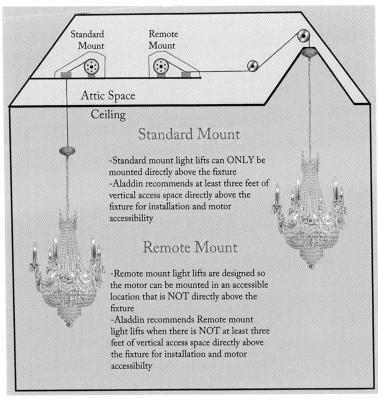

The Aladdin Light Lift is a switch-activated remote pulley that puts a chandelier within reach for servicing.

LED strips are used inventively to direct light on a minimalist foyer and the main entrance to a living room. *Photo courtesy of KLUS*

architectural detail, or a special piece of furniture, careful accent lighting needs to be considered.

When developing a whole-house lighting plan, the entry hall may not be your first consideration, but it always deserves attention. Safety, access, movement, and perhaps some drama should be the prime motivating factors—along with a need to introduce the basics of your entire home-decorating plan.

Creative lighting can lead you through spaces. Here, indirect wall lighting and lights under a floating console create a welcoming foyer while highlighting the interior architecture. Design by Jennifer Post. *Photograph: Antoine Bootz*

Hallway Lighting Tips

• To draw the eye down the hall, place lights close to either end of the corridor and a minimum of 8 feet apart.

• A specialty light near the end of the hallway will pull you forward.

• Sconces should be placed high on the wall to draw your eye up and make the passage feel less claustrophobic. In a tight hallway, hang fixtures slightly above head height.

• If your hall has a high ceiling, make an impact with suspended lights or a chandelier.

• If ceiling height is limited, recessed ceiling lights can be a good solution.

• Hallway lighting should be proportional to the space. If your hallway is large, pendant lights need to be substantial. But in a small entranceway, oversized lighting could impede movement through that space.

• After lighting is installed, check for dark spots by standing at one end of the hall. A well-lit passageway will be evenly lit.

• A range of different light sources will make the space feel richer and allow for mood changes within the hallway.

• Consider lampshade color if you're using shaded pendants. Pale colorways allow light to pass through; dark colors may impede light, making the space feel somber.

• For entrance hallways, select shades or fixtures that create a dramatic effect by casting light patterns on the ceiling.

• To add elegance, opt for wall lamps that project light evenly up and down.

• To eliminate dark areas, light stair landings that are visible from an entry hall.

• To show off a display of decorative accessories on a hall table or surface, add a table lamp that emits a soft pool of light.

• For a traditional look, place a matching pair of lamps on either end of a slender hall console.

• Stairs with more than six treads require light switches at both ends of the stair, unless motion sensors are used or stair lights are always on.

• To ensure hallway safety, add light wherever a level change occurs.

• Be creative in layering the light. Hallways are as important as any other spaces in your home.

Layered lighting illuminates a home office that hardly looks like one. Utilizing traditional lighting techniques, a task lamp illuminates the work surface, and a collection of lamps provides the ambient lighting. The wall-hung bookcase adorned with collectibles includes numerous decorative lamps to provide interest. A massive painting lit by a picture light creates a stunning backdrop. Design by David Scott Interiors. *Photographer: Antoine Bootz*

Versatility in a Home Office

There are two kinds of light—the glow that illuminates and the glare that obscures.
—James Thurber, author, humorist, cartoonist

A home office is a room with a purpose. While everyday household management tasks can probably be done at the kitchen table, if you work from home, your office must incorporate aspects of a commercial space to ensure high productivity. To complicate matters, home offices often double as other spaces, such as a guest room or laundry room, so the lighting must be flexible.

What are your home office requirements? The kind of work you do will determine the lighting plan. Will you be doing paperwork, working primarily at the computer, or reading books? Maybe you need space to spread out material swatches or paint chips. If so, the color temperature of your light source will be particularly relevant. If you are sitting at a computer screen all day, the need to illuminate it properly will shape the lighting choices you make. Improper or inadequate room lighting not only compromises your vision but also results in fatigue and lack of focus.

Task lighting is a top consideration. It will alleviate eye strain, a major component of workplace fatigue. Task lighting should be aimed to your left if you're right handed, and to the right if you're left-handed. Either way, the point is not to create shadows, so the light should be directed toward you. An adjustable fixture is the best choice for task light. This could be a wall-mounted swing-arm fixture or one with an articulated arm that you can shift to, say, find a file in a drawer.

For secondary lighting, a sconce or two or a desktop lamp can reinforce the visual character of the space. Look for fixtures that coordinate with those in the rest of your home. I have both stationary and adjustable lights—task lighting to focus on whatever I'm doing and indirect lighting positioned to shine upward, its beams bouncing off the ceiling, thus eliminating shadows as well as indirectly lighting my work.

Illumination must be color-balanced. Choose bulbs with the same color temperature to avoid lows or highs in light output. Either would be disturbing, because the eye is attracted to the brightest light. For example, don't install 2700K in a desk lamp and 3000K in an overhead fixture. My Connecticut home has

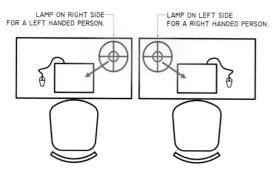

Desk lighting should be positioned opposite the user's dominant hand, so that the light shines directly on the work without casting a shadow.

tunable-white, warm, dimmable LED lighting throughout, and I am aware that when the lights are dimmed, their beams become more amber. You wouldn't want that effect in a home office. Instead, choose lights that retain their original color when dimmed. This is known as usable white light. Where focused work occurs, consistent color temperature is key.

Cooler color temperatures are best for home offices. Although 2700K is the standard color temperature for general home use because of its warmth, I would opt instead for 3000K in a home office. Brighter in intensity and higher in tone, it will keep you much more alert.

Note that no matter what kind of work you plan to do in your home office, augment task lighting with other types of lighting: table lamps placed beside or near you as accents, for example. They'll add an element of visual warmth that makes your workspace feel homier, even if it's just a corner of your kitchen or a small desk at the back of the laundry room.

Unlikely as it seems, there is wisdom in claiming part of a laundry room as your home office. For one thing, it is usually quiet, since people don't hang out there. For another, the task-oriented lighting will probably be favorable, if not particularly flattering, but that is not the point in a workspace.

I have known more than one homeowner who carved an office out of an unused closet—to be sure, it was walk-in size or at least a two-rod depth. The beauty of such an arrangement is that when you are finished working, you simply turn off the lights, shut the doors, and the office disappears! To light it appropriately, I suggest installing two recessed lights or two surface-mounted fixtures, one on either end of the work surface and focused on the surface.

A tunable-white LED lighting strip installed in the ceiling can make you feel alert when tuned to 6000K, and more relaxed when lit by only 2000K. *Photo courtesy of PureEdge Lighting*

Turning a closet into an office makes smart use of space; here the lighting is selected and placed to make the space feel larger, less confining. Design by Dorothy Claud Interiors: Heaton Place. Lighting design by David Shepherd–Tazz Lighting, Inc. Product supplier: Tazz Lighting, Inc.

The Ceiling Option

When desktop or table space is minimal, or if adding a floor lamp would cramp a space, overhead track lighting is a good solution because it is adjustable. Mount the tracks about 20 inches away from the wall in front of you, and position the light source so it doesn't create glare. Adding an accessory such as an eggcrate louver or other type of diffuser will eliminate glare.

If placed appropriately, these fixtures can do double duty, providing ambient light for the wall in front of you as well as task lighting. Be sure the beams projected from those fixtures are directed toward the forward edge of your work surface, just as you would when illuminating a kitchen. Putting light in a home office is actually quite similar to the challenge you'd face in a kitchen, where you're preparing food and reading recipes, sometimes from books or magazines, other times on an iPAD.

Consider the Sun

As with any room in the house, you'll want to take advantage of sunlight because it's so energy efficient. Harness that light so it enhances how you work in the space. Natural light can be a blessing or a curse, however, and sometimes it's a little of each. So consider sunshine a variable. On cloudy or stormy days, it may be only a whisper and not particularly useful. On clear days, the light level fluctuates, predictably rising and falling as the sun moves across the sky. So if a home office includes a generous window, you'll have to compensate for the sun's impact on sunny days and its loss at night or on cloudy days. Remember that the goal is to create a consistent light level.

Don't ignore the threat of glare, particularly in a room where you spend a great many hours. In a space graced with large windows, you'll be challenged to prevent glaring light from pouring into the room at various times. Before ordering your fixtures, observe how natural light affects the space. The amount of glare depends on the time of year, the part of the world you live in, and whether your office has a northern or southern exposure. The logical solution is to install a pull-down shade that diffuses sunlight rather than blocking it out entirely.

Where to place the desk? Some people want their desk to face a window so they can view their garden or keep an eye on kids playing outside. Others prefer having their back to a window, so they can look into the room or avoid outdoor distractions. A third option is to angle the desk 90 degrees from the window, so sunlight pouring in will cross your right or left shoulder before hitting the work surface.

Also be aware that you don't want to see a light fixture reflected in your computer screen. So, the furniture arrangement may determine the placement of your light source, whether it's mainly from an overhead fixture, an adjustable wall mount, or an adjustable tabletop lamp.

When window light is inadequate, or if your home office sits directly under the eaves, consider cutting into the ceiling and installing a skylight to bring in natural light from above. To soften direct sunlight at certain times of day, consider adding a remote-controlled shade. That way the room is never flooded with light, even when the sun is directly overhead.

I've had clients who are up very early or work late in the day to communicate with people in distant parts of the world. In accommodating radically different time zones, they have to clue their body to stay awake and alert. Lighting can provide major assistance. In those cases we install both a blackout roller shade and a decorative-fabric shade, with an LED strip at the top of the window between the two. I recommend having controls that simulate conditions on the basis of the time of day and the outdoor weather.

A great many factors influence the location and design of a home office. Regardless of its size or placement, sensitive lighting can remove some of the stress, creating both an efficient and an interesting place in which to function.

Home Office Lighting Tips

• Utilize natural light, but be mindful of glare, especially from your computer screen, and augment it with artificial light to support an "anytime" work schedule.

• Overhead lighting can create glare and shadows, so layer the output with good task and ambient lighting.

• A higher, or cooler, light temperature helps with alertness and productivity; 3000K is ideal.

• For task lighting, select an adjustable fixture or one that has good articulation so you can focus the light where needed.

• If a space has workstations for different tasks (viewing art or a computer screen, for example), light them accordingly. Different tasks may require different color temperatures (K).

• Choose light sources with a CRI of at least 90, which shows materials and objects in their truest colors.

• Insufficient lumen output can cause eye strain and fatigue. Be sure you have 800 lumens per fixture.

• In addition to satisfying ambient and task lighting requirements, add decorative and accent lighting for visual appeal—it will make you feel good in the space.

• To reduce the effect of glare from a computer screen, place LED strip lighting behind the computer. You can buy strip lights specifically for this purpose. Be thoughtful about how and where you position permanent fixtures.

• To prevent shadows, remember that if you're right-handed, task lighting must be on the left; if you are left-handed, place it on the right.

• Distance from a task light to a work surface should be approximately 15½ inches, depending on the fixture.

• Consider adding a tunable white lightbulb to a lamp, one that can be controlled by a mobile device. Softly colored light can be extremely soothing in a workplace environment.

• Optimize your workspace by using pendant lights or sconces with articulating arms, so that surfaces can be kept clear.

• If your home office has bookshelves, consider illuminating them to add interest and depth.

CEILING

WINDOW
CEILING

3"± 2³⁄₄"± 2¹⁄₂"±

WINDOW WALL

ROLLER SHADE
(BLACKOUT)

LED LIGHT STRIP

FIXED ROMAN SHADE

To enhance home-office productivity, either night or day, and no matter how much sunlight shines in, an LED strip light with diffuser is mounted in front of a privacy roller shade but behind the window treatment. The ceiling fixtures supply ambient lighting. Design by Pavarini Design, Inc. *Photograph: © Marco Ricca Studio*

CHAPTER 10
Backyards and Beyond

More and more, so it seems to me, light is the beautifier of the building.
—Frank Lloyd Wright, architect

Outdoor lighting at the edge of a patio brings safety, security, and nighttime drama to a backyard setting. In addition, LED strip lighting and recessed fixtures point up the house's architecture.

Too often an afterthought, outdoor lighting deserves as much consideration as that in a living room or kitchen. Safety and security are top considerations: you don't want anyone to risk injury when negotiating pathways and other outdoor areas, either because they are underlit or blindingly illuminated at night. However, you'll also want to light your home's architecture, landscaping, and welcoming features. Creative exterior lighting can work wonders for any property, turning trees and foliage into sculpture. Up-lighting trees with well lights and hanging pierced moon lights from high branches creates magical effects after dark.

There are four distinct aspects of exterior lighting: the lighting design, the acquisition of fixtures, the installation of fixtures, and, finally, maintenance. Also essential is a control system that can be set to turn lights on and off.

Low-voltage systems, which consume one-tenth the power of 120-volt indoor systems, are typically used outdoors. LEDs can be up to three times as bright as their incandescent predecessors and have proved capable of enduring dramatic weather shifts and extreme temperature changes. Because they can deliver up to 100,000 hours of efficient illumination, they are likely to last up to four times longer than their predecessors and thus rarely require replacement.

Where hardy white halogens were once the preferred exterior lighting sources, LEDs have effectively supplanted them. Not only are they energy efficient and dimmable, but integrated RGBs allow their colors to be changed remotely and instantly—creating festive seasonal lighting. All of these advances make it less challenging to point up a home's exterior beauty while ensuring the safety of people moving about the property.

Keeping night skies dark. More and more communities are now mandating outdoor lighting products approved by the International Dark Sky Association (IDA). They minimize glare, light trespass, and night-sky pollution. If you have ever tried sourcing architectural-quality IDA-approved light fixtures, however, you know they aren't easy to find. Many outdoor lights marketed as dark-sky-friendly don't carry the IDA certification seal and are likely to fail inspection after the lights are installed. So be patient—and shop carefully.

Here, as it would be anywhere, proper lighting installation is essential. It's really important.

Areas of Focus

Outdoor lighting should address the driveway and garage, walkways and steps, exterior doorways, decks and patios, trees, landscaping, and any special architectural or water features. Before developing the plan, do a detailed walk-around—on a dark, mostly moonless evening—with a strong-beamed flashlight in hand. That's how you can begin to pinpoint potential trouble spots and identify landscape or architectural features to highlight. And do be mindful of neighbors—you don't want to light their property.

Truly dark skies are a rarity nowadays, except in remote areas; light pollution continues to create distractions from our planet's natural beauty.

Pay special attention to driveways and garages, to ensure smooth access when driving to and from your home. Whether you mount lights in neighboring trees or just light the path from the driveway to garage, your objective should be to provide convenience and safety—that is, uninterrupted lighting without glare. Installing a lantern-like fixture on a post at the head of the driveway is an effective way to mark the driveway. Wiring such a fixture could be costly, however, so you may want to install so-called filter lights, each powered by a photometric or solar-powered cell. This type of installation is both economical and flexible. Because it is wireless, the fixture could be mounted on a stake secured in the ground, wherever you wish, as long as they have adequate exposure to sunlight.

In my experience, solar-powered LEDs produce lighting that's a little bit dimmer than hardwired alternatives. However, even if the emitted light is just a relatively soft glow, the driveway entrance will be evident. Now available are solar-powered outdoor LED fixtures in a variety of designs and configurations. I use solar LED torches for gardens and paths. The corncob solar LED lamp inside is programmed to flicker and glow like a real flame and last for years.

Note, however, that the driveway itself should also be lit. For convenience, driveway and garage lighting can be linked to a timer, or sensor, which you can set or control remotely from your mobile device so that the light turns on at sundown and off at dawn, or at whatever time you wish. A more convenient and energy-savvy move would be to link the lights to a motion sensor programmed to switch lights on only when the area is in use.

Some homes have a porte cochere—a covered vehicle entrance, usually at the side of a home, where passengers can be "delivered" without being exposed to the elements. Here, a decorative outdoor fixture, suitable to the style of the residence, is appropriate. It will add to the warm, welcoming feeling you'll probably want to express. If your home's architecture is contemporary, for example, you could choose nondecorative or architecturally based fixtures—very simple, very clean.

Walkway and stair lighting should be subtle—you won't want any outdoor walkway to look like a spotlighted runway. Consider staggering the light placement from one side to the other, rather than having equal rows of opposing fixtures. Shaded-tier and mushroom-shaped fixtures and bollard lights can be installed close to the ground, shedding light low on a walkway or vegetation. And, of course, you can also find LEDs designed to be embedded in a walkway or in fixtures shaped like bricks or pavers, topped with an unbreakable plastic lens.

Path lights along outdoor steps are important safety considerations, while spotlights and well lights add to after-dark ambience by focusing on plantings and giving the landscape an overall immersive quality. *Photo courtesy of Oregon Outdoor Lighting*

Moonlight Effect

As with interior installations, exterior lighting can be multidimensional, but it must be layered sensitively so that it provides ample illumination without creating patches of glare. For me, the challenge is to draw inspiration from the moon, rather than the sun. Just as the effect of indoor lighting is largely a replication of sunlight, exterior lighting should achieve the warm-white effect of moonbeams. Because moonlight has always been referred to as "romantic light," make sure your outdoor lighting choices emulate that feeling.

This can be a delicate balance to achieve, because you want to avoid ultrawhite light, with its low CRI and high color temperature, sometimes known as "ghost lighting." The ideal temperature is around 3000K, which means it can still exude a bit of a warmish glow. Further up the scale, 3000K to 3500K, the effect will be a cooler, whiter light. Unlike inside a house, shadows are desirable—playing up tree leaves and limbs or architectural features that cast interesting patterns.

Materials

LEDs are widely used in outdoor spotlights, floodlights, path lights, and sconces and overheads, plus lights that are integrated with Bluetooth speakers and bug zappers. With any of these choices, the lighting must be wired and installed properly, which will also make ongoing maintenance easier. The lighting must be shielded from the elements. Every exterior light fixture must be encased in some kind of covering, not just to protect it from dirt but mainly from moisture. Because a lightbulb is sealed, fully contained in its own envelope, it's effectively waterproof, but the connection to the electrical source must also be shielded. And this must be emphasized: when selecting appropriate outdoor fixtures, corrosion resistance should always be a major concern.

High humidity, salty air, and the sun's UV rays all have a huge impact on how long and how well outdoor light fixtures can withstand exposure to the elements before corrosion sets in. We've all seen faded outdoor fixtures covered in chalky white powder; similar to accumulated iron rust. This is what happens to aluminum when it oxidizes, and it can occur after even one season of exposure to the elements. The dirty little secret about decorative outdoor lighting is that it rarely looks as good as it did on the day it was installed.

Resisting or delaying oxidation. One effective way to ensure durability is to install corrosion-resistant products. This means making sure that every piece of equipment you choose has been pretreated thoroughly

with a corrosion-inhibiting finish. Properly pretreated and finished, aluminum can withstand the harshest, most-punishing climates.

I have learned that prior to assembly, all components of the outdoor fixtures marketed by Hammerton Studio have been separately pretreated and finished, thus eliminating microscopic voids that can trap corrosion-causing moisture. Their fixtures have a rugged AMAA powder coat finish, the same quality and grade of finish regularly used on aluminum-clad skyscrapers. AMAA is an acronym for the American Architectural Manufacturers Association, which rates finishes according to how much UV protection they provide and how well their color and gloss resist corrosion and weathering. Because this finish contains no volatile organic compounds (VOCs), its use contributes to LEED (Leadership in Energy and Environmental Design) credits.

For ongoing maintenance:

• Make sure that no tree limb, plant growth, or shrub is obscuring any outdoor fixtures, thus potentially blocking the light.

• Examine each outdoor-fixture mount to make sure it's still secure and safe—and not threatening any present or future plant growth (over time, inclement weather can cause fixtures to shift and become unfocused).

• Keep outdoor fixtures and lenses clean and use a lime-removing household cleaner to eliminate calcium deposits from rainwater that may accumulate and obscure the light.

• Lubricate lamp bases and sockets with a high-heat silicone compound from your hardware store or lumberyard. This will prevent corrosion, which makes lightbulbs challenging to unscrew. Also, take time to apply an antiseize/antioxidizing lubricant to all socket threads.

• Check out the IP rating. It signals the degree of ingress protection an outdoor lighting installation has. Simply stated, the IP rating will indicate how well a particular exterior fixture is protected against the intrusion of dirt, dust, or liquid—dampness, mainly, but rainfall and snow also have an impact. The ideal rating for a typical outdoor lighting installation is IP65. If you're concerned about how well a particular fixture will resist very heavy rainfall, that number needs to be IP66. When you shop, you'll find the IP rating printed on the fixture itself.

• Check the UL rating; it too is indicated on the product or on its packaging. Underwriters Laboratories is an independent product-safety organization whose routine testing reveals how products comply with nationally recognized safety standards. Here are two relevant examples:

Outdoor fixtures designed to be embedded in hardscape surfaces are available in various sizes. *Photo courtesy of Focus Industries, Inc.*

UL Damp is a rating that means a fixture is suitable for moist and humid situations but should not be exposed directly to rain or snow. Partly covered installations under canopies or covered porches fit this category.

UL Wet is a rating for installations on open porches, pergolas, open walkways, and uncovered gazebos, where exposure to rain, snow, or ocean spray is likely.

FOCUS INDUSTRIES

Design

To design with light is to dictate what the viewer will experience. The challenge is to plan for overall illumination, task lighting, and accent lighting. If there are outbuildings or a pool house, their illumination will add richness to the design.

Stairs. When lighting a set of steps, if you are working with all-new construction, you can arrange to have illumination embedded under the lip of each step. A less expensive alternative for any kind of project is strip lighting or rope lighting, which is usually waterproof. Regardless of lighting type, make sure it is embedded in a way that it's hazard free and hidden from daytime view. Embedding lights directly into a set of steps is usually preferable to an above-surface mount that could cause someone to trip. Glare, too, can cause a misstep when light is installed on top of a surface.

Exterior doorways. Walkways and steps usually end at a doorway that needs to be lit. If it's a front door, good lighting is key to identifying the primary entrance for visitors and ensuring safe passage. Good lighting not only helps people locate the keyhole or doorbell at night; it also adds a welcoming touch.

Lights flanking the doorway and installed about a quarter of the way down from the top of the door will ensure easy access—as will lanterns with tinted, frosted, or seeded lenses that prevent glare. While compact fluorescents (CFLs) were once recommended here to replace incandescent bulbs, longer-lasting LEDs are now the popular choice.

Patios and decks. The challenge is bringing the inside out—that is, creating a compatible extension of the interior design choices. On a porch, you would install ceiling fixtures or wall mounts that enhance the architectural style of the home or replicate the design choices you've made indoors. Options for lighting a patio can include outdoor-ready fixtures mounted on a sidewall of the house or garage—whichever abuts the patio. Or it might include weatherproof lighting mounted in surrounding trees, shrubs, or gardens.

At my stone house in Connecticut, I installed new patios made of stone embedded in concrete. Before pouring any material, I identified the exterior aspects I wanted to illuminate—the patios, plus some of the stone facade and surrounding plantings. Before any material was laid, I had all the essential conduits positioned so I could imbed LED up-lights in the patios. Each light is adjustable, which means I can remove the lenses and refocus the beam of light as desired.

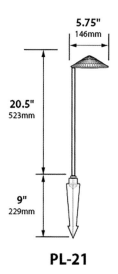

PL-21

A path light can also be used to illuminate low-growing plants within your garden beds, and when specifying, you'll find a variety of canopy styles, each of which can add nuance to the fixtures you choose. *Photo courtesy of Focus Industries, Inc.*

And rather than using directional, bullet-style fixtures that will inevitably obstruct plant growth, I installed decorative lights on the patio edges that are stem-mounted, elevating the light source so its beams are directed down onto the plantings.

Self-lighting furniture is another attractive option for patios. A penthouse rooftop our firm designed included cube tables that light up. They lend a festive atmosphere, including RGB lights in different colors for use on special occasions. Another alternative is to simply install warm-white lights that approximate moonlight.

While the purpose of lighting a deck or patio is to entice people to sit outside on a balmy night, the truth is that evil is always lurking—bugs, and they are attracted to bright light. You can try to avoid them by mounting or hanging lights high overhead, illuminating outdoor activities with candles or hurricane lamps, or investing in bug-deflecting LED lights purchased online or at a home center store. I suggest you experiment to see what works best in your area.

LEDs can light outdoor furniture subtly and creatively. *Photo courtesy of VONDOM*

A tree-hung LED pendant focuses light downward through a star-point accent, one of many perforated sleeve-pattern styles designed to cast light directly into a tree canopy. The fixture is lit by a 3-watt, 170-lumen, 2700K LED module with a projected 35,000-hour life. *Photo courtesy of Dreamscape Lighting*

Trees and landscaping. Highlighting trees can be a beautiful way to showcase an exterior setting. Tree leaves provide a bounce of light, and deciduous trees can be treated as architecture. You can light them from below—from shallow well lights in the ground—or from within the tree branches—"moonlights" hung on upper limbs and directed downward. Moonlights are typically cylinder shaped and pierced to create a decorative effect with pinpoints of light.

Let understatement guide you. Overlighting will have a negative effect, producing glare and ultimately flattening the perspective. It could also focus light where you don't want it—back into the house or into the homes of unappreciative neighbors. This is one reason dimmable exterior lighting is recommended.

Depth perception. Lighting trees or outbuildings that are some distance from the house creates an expanded sense of depth and interest. Wiring a property can be challenging, of course, but there are solar-powered exterior LED fixtures that require no batteries or electrical connections, allowing them to be placed literally anywhere. The only requirement is that the solar panels receive direct sunlight at least five hours a day.

Battery-operated fixtures are another godsend that allow light to be placed anywhere. In Connecticut, I have a battery-operated standing lamp with a lampshade that sits next to an outdoor sofa. The light has a glass cover that screws into the fixture, and a gasket keeps out moisture.

On one project, our firm lit a terrace with what can only be described as a doughnut of LED light. About 5 feet in diameter, it is equipped with RGB and changes color as desired. We positioned it in the garden, but because it's battery powered, it can be moved anywhere easily. Battery-powered lights—also made for tables, planters, and benches—consist of dense plastic and weather-sealed lamps, so they won't need to be rescued from a rainstorm.

Lighting controls. A lighting-control system installed in my Arizona house is linked to two exterior lights that are programmed to turn on at dusk and off at dawn, or I can control them through my phone or tablet. I save energy by being able to limit their operation to only the most-essential times. This can also be achieved with plug-in timers. Unlike hardwired switches, they don't need to be installed by a professional electrician.

A pergola is dramatically illuminated with integrated LEDs.

Pools, ponds, and water features. Lit water features can produce subtle or dramatic nighttime effects. Aside from the fact that swimming at night in a heated pool is every kid's dream, lighting your pool will enhance your entire property. Rippling water reflecting off tree canopies and shrubbery is truly mesmerizing. Battery-operated resin spheres with RGBs are a great choice for use in ponds and pools.

Pool lighting is required for safety as well as decorative reasons. Most pool packages include basic lighting options that may warrant upgrading. What about colored lights? Or lights that rotate colors as a result of a clever timing device? These are available in various shapes and an entire rainbow of color changes. Keep in mind that fixtures rated for aquatic use can also be installed in ponds, fountains, and waterfalls, bringing the underwater world alive with the click of a switch.

My house has no pool, but the property backs up to a serene lake. To light the water nearest the shore, I floated a fixture that looks like a lamp with a shade on it. What keeps it afloat and prevents it from toppling is a ballast, which is invisible below the waterline. Because it looks like a floating lamp, visitors do a double-take, particularly on very dark nights, but there's really nothing fanciful about it. The fixture is lit by waterproof housing, an entirely practical installation.

Architectural assets. Well-designed outdoor lighting can point up your home's architectural features, just as it does inside. Features such as exposed framing on eaves and interesting surface textures all are fair game. Just make sure the fixtures are pretreated for exterior use.

A home's exterior walls, pillars, fences, gates, and any additional structures on the property all present their own textures. For example, a graze of surface lighting accentuates a brick or stone exterior and the shadows those materials create. To achieve dramatic nighttime effects on my boathouse in Connecticut, I installed up-lighting that not only enhances the texture of the stone walls but illuminates the soffits from underneath. These fixtures are mounted about 6 inches away from the vertical surfaces, so the foot-deep eaves are adequately illuminated. Alternatively, recessed lighting could be installed in a soffit to effectively downwash the facade.

An LED-lit waterfall cascades from the roof overhang into the pool of this luxury home in the American Southwest. Path lights mark the landscape perimeter, and recessed lighting illuminates the patio under the overhang. *Photo courtesy of Robinette Architects*

Outdoor Lighting Tips

• Three basic categories of lighting apply to the outdoors: ambient, task, and, for drama and interest, accent lighting.

• A critical look at your property in daylight will help shape your nighttime outdoor vision.

• For energy conservation and future maintenance, use LEDs on all exterior lighting. Maintain consistent kelvins and CRIs in your lamping and strive to achieve a warm glow.

• For doorways, paths, and walkways, focus on safety and security first.

• Pay special attention to the main entrance so people will know where to enter.

• Vary the lighting plan with an eye to creating depth and interest.

• Entertainment areas may call both for subtle and dramatic lighting. Fire pits and torches lend a sense of romance.

• Shadows and dark areas can add interest, depth, and drama.

• Exploit the fact that trees make beautiful nighttime features, whether bathed with floodlights (approximate beam spread: 120 degrees), spotlights (approximate beam spread: 45 degrees), or tree-mounted light fixtures.

• Light a pond, pool, stream, or other water feature with aboveground spots or washes of light. Lit waterfalls cast beautiful ripples of light on surrounding areas.

• Unless you are working with an LED outdoor lighting system, you could be faced with this problem: linking several fixtures to one cable in a daisy chain can overpower the lights closest to your transformer, leaving the last fixture in the lineup power-starved and dim.

• If you keep your cable runs under 50 feet, power should arrive at light fixtures in their sweet spot: 8 to 15 volts for LEDs, or 10.8 to 11.5 volts for halogens.

• When focusing outdoor lights, be sensitive to your neighbors. Avoid light pollution and don't blind them with direct light or glare.

Embedded in a patio, well lights up-light a home's eaves and throw the stone walls into relief. The soaring tree canopy benefits from the residual light. Design by Pavarini Design, Inc. *Photographer: J. Randall Tarasuk*

True Tech

Light has not just intensity, but also a vibration, which is capable of roughening a smooth material, of giving a three-dimensional quality to a flat surface.
—Renzo Piano, architect

Excellent LED lighting can start with far more colorful ideas.

LIGHT-EMITTING DIODE

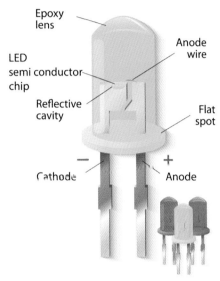

All the components of a minuscule LED diode appear in this diagram.

This chapter is intended to help readers dig a little deeper into LED technology and how to apply it. The goal is to help you choose fixtures with confidence on the basis of the product labeling that manufacturers provide, and also to spark your creativity.

First, keep in mind that LEDs, or light-emitting diodes, resemble tiny lightbulbs linked to an electrical circuit. Unlike incandescent bulbs, which cause a filament to glow, LED illumination results from the movement of electrons within a semiconductor material. These have a very long life span, nearly equal to that of a standard transistor— 50,000 hours or more. And their efficiency (also called efficacy) in lumens per watt output is considerably more than traditional Edison incandescent lighting. But they consume 20 to 30 percent less energy than comparable fluorescent choices.

While their heat output is much less than incandescent lighting, they do emit some warmth. Thus they require passive cooling via a thermal-transfer device, or what we call a heat sink, which draws warmth away and keeps these devices relatively cool. Depending on the amount of heat the LEDs generate, heat sinks vary in size and must be attached to the back of every LED semiconductor, to draw warmth away from the diodes. Manufacturers do this in a variety of ways.

A driver is needed to control LEDs. It tells LEDs when to turn on or off, and at what intensity. Drivers vary in size and technology, and that affects how the LED illuminates, how it dims, and how it performs overall. LED retrofit lamps (which fit into traditional incandescent-bulb sockets) and chip-on-board products have integral drivers installed by the manufacturer. In contrast, LED products, such as tape lighting and those driven by a remote driver, provide information on suggested drivers in their product literature so that you can make your own selection.

It's important to realize that with LED technology, you have a choice to make about the LED color best

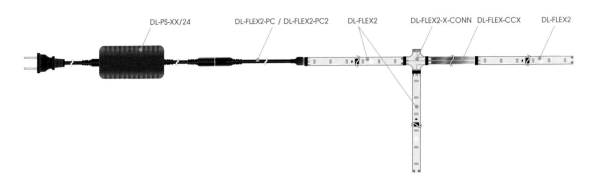

The diagram illustrates the makeup of a typical LED strip-lighting setup: a driver with an A/C plug plus connectors and a flexible LED strip. *Photo courtesy of Jesco Lighting*

suited to an installation, and you get what you pay for when you select a driver. Good drivers offer extensive options such as dimming to 1 percent smoothly and effectively for ten years or more, while lesser drivers often have flaws such as blinking, erratic dimming, or a reduced life.

One of the challenges in residential lighting is how color is addressed. In theory, there is no such thing as a white LED. Because an LED's natural glow is bluish, a coating of yellow phosphorus is applied to each diode to offset that blue tone—so that the projected LED color can shift mainly to white. The earliest LED bulbs and fixtures, which notably emitted that bluish glow, were superseded by refinements that now enable them to

emit the warm-white tones suitable to residential environments. We can now purchase warm-dim options that become warmer as you dim them because they feature parallel LEDs: one that fades out and another that fades to a pale yellow or orange before turning off, replicating the effect of the Edison incandescent bulb.

This technology works out well if you have an antique chandelier and are eager to maintain an Old World look by using retrofit lamping: you can light the chandelier at a low color temperature compatible with that of a glowing filament (2200K). It will supply the traditional feeling of classic Edison lightbulbs—and also keep that fixture glowing for tens of thousands of hours without relamping.

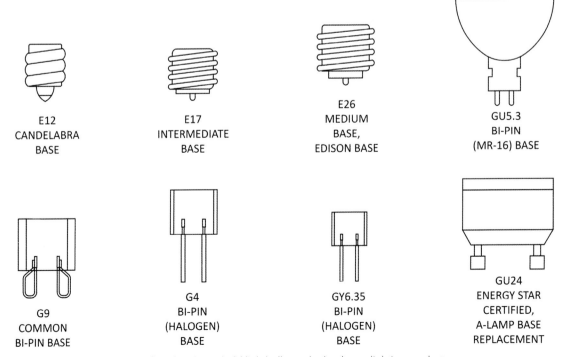

These common base types are found on household lightbulbs and other home lighting products.

Rating or Energy Output

LED bulbs are manufactured both for indoor and outdoor applications and are rated the same way as other lighting fixtures. The UL (Underwriters Laboratories) listing assures us they meet established standards of quality and safety for use at home. I think it best to purchase only UL-approved products when choosing LEDs.

- UL Damp–listed LEDs are recommended where humidity levels are high.
- UL Wet–listed LEDs are for use in outdoor or in sealed, submersible light fixtures.
- Other ratings include output (in lumens) and color kelvins (K), to be discussed later in this chapter.

LED products are often Energy Star Certified, which means they're guaranteed to meet major energy-saving thresholds. To receive Energy Star certification, a product must consume 70 to 80 percent less energy than incandescent alternatives, last ten to twenty-five times longer, and save considerable amounts of money over the product's lifetime of use. They must also produce 70 to 90 percent less heat, making them safer and less costly in terms of air-conditioning. Like other Energy Star products, high-quality LEDs are tested rigorously by independent labs to uphold testing standardization and achieve unbiased results. I highly recommend Energy Star Certified LED products, not only for their energy savings but also for the three-year warranties such products must carry. Many LED products are warrantied for five years or more.

The Color Advantage

Color is an important topic when LED technology is discussed. Pros talk about the color temperature of LED light in terms of correlated color temperature (CCT), which is measured in degrees of kelvin (K is a unit of measure for absolute temperature). Just as those bluish flames emanating from your gas grill reliably reflect the ultrahigh temperatures required to cook most foods, this blue light also has a very high color temperature.

As noted earlier, white LEDs are intrinsically blue and thus cool in color temperature, possibly reaching 5000K or more, before the manufacturer uses phosphors to correct the color—to "warm" the light being emitted. Very warm light, such as that produced by a candle, is much lower in color temperature, falling to around 1850K. For comfort, LED lighting for esidential use should register within the "warm" range of 2700K to 3000K.

While still somewhat cooler than traditional Edison bulbs giving off 2400K, that range is considered to fall within an acceptable realm of comfort, and manufacturers can produce it reliably.

CCT range is broader in commercial applications whose needs require greater stimulus: areas where brighter and whiter light is appropriate. Installations of over 3000K turn up in hotel lobbies, reception areas, and supermarkets. Installations of over 3500K can be found in offices, classrooms, large stores, and showrooms, where people are expected to be alert and focused. Light whose CCT reaches 5000K is most appropriate in dental offices, hospitals, and clinics, where highly technical work such as surgical procedures takes place. A CCT of 6000K or more is evident in jewelry-store displays, beauty salons, art galleries, museums, and printing facilities needing to replicate the pure white of daylight. Of course, any lighting product you acquire for home use should be around 3000K for large public areas and at most 2700K for intimate spaces—bedrooms and other locations where people sleep or simply chill out.

Note, too, that the color-rendering index (CRI) measures how true colors of materials and objects will appear—that is, how discernible the colors in a room are under a particular light source. The scale is from 0 to 100, zero meaning terrible and 100 meaning perfect. Have you ever noticed how difficult it can be to locate an object in your car in a parking lot at night? That's because such facilities are equipped with efficient high-pressure sodium lighting that has such a low color temperature—a CRI of only 24, for example. At such a low CRI, color is rendered within an extremely narrow range, making it nearly impossible to experience its full impact. That's why you may find it nearly impossible to distinguish black from gray or blue, or even green, under lighting with such a low value.

For residential interiors, where my staff and I need to pay close attention to how textiles and finishes appear, anything under a CRI of 85 will greatly compromise paint color, fabric, and furnishings choices—even the quality of artwork we want to display. In such situations, I recommend purchasing LED lighting with a CRI of 90 or above, now that manufacturers are capable of reaching the level of color accuracy that will justify the investment you've made—so your home's interior will always look as you want it to, and never feel disappointingly dull or anemic.

An additional value you may find in product literature or on product packaging is the R9 value of red. That also determines the color output of an LED but is a more complex topic than we'll deal with here. When given the option, I suggest you stick with LED products advertised for an R9 value greater than 20 to achieve successful color rendition.

Lightbulb packaging takes different forms, depending on its manufacturer. But typical labeling lists lumen output, color temperature, base size, and wattage consumption.

Lighting-Label Lore

The Federal Trade Commission has mandated that every LED bulb be accurately labeled so you can easily discern its properties and performance before making a purchase. You'll find the lighting-facts label on the side or the rear panel. The label should include the following data for each bulb in the package:

- **light output,** noted as "brightness," in average lumens rounded off to the nearest five
- **estimated energy cost** per year—computed as the "estimated yearly energy" cost and based on the average initial wattage, a usage rate of three hours per day and eleven cents per kilowatt-hour
- **estimated life span**—as expressed in years, rounded to the nearest tenth and based on a rate of three hours of use per day
- **light appearance,** the correlated color temperature (CCT) of each bulb in the package. This is measured in degrees kelvin and expressed by a number and a marker placed on a scale ranging from 2600K (warm) on the left to 6600K (cool) on the right.
- **energy used** refers to the wattage consumption of the lamp.
- **the Energy Star logo** indicates that the manufacturer is in compliance with performance standards set by the US Department of Energy and the US Environmental Protection Agency.

LED Nitty-Gritty

The chart on page 125 compares LED lumen output to wattages used in long-familiar incandescent bulbs. Since LEDs consume comparatively few watts, lumens are often used as the standard measure of brightness.

When exploring LED technology and product availability, I think you'll find few negatives. Everyday advances are resulting in LEDs that exponentially expand the realm of lighting possibilities. Of course, since LEDs need DC low voltage, every LED device requires a driver to convert 120 volts from the electrical source to the LED bulb or fixture. LED bulbs hide the driver at their base, and LED fixtures use a driver integral to the LED fixture or remotely mounted. They may require a step-down device to convert 120 volts from the electrical source for use in an LED bulb or fixture.

Because LEDs consume comparatively little electricity, too much electric power will burn them out, a common occurrence in traditional lighting design. Halogen light sources such as track lighting, which utilizes MR-16 bulbs, have always required a step-down transformer to convert an electrical box's 120-volt capacity to the needs of light fixtures running at only 12 volts. LEDs are more individually specific, requiring a driver that converts electric current to exactly what the LED modules need. This depends on the electronic

BRIGHTNESS IN LUMENS	220+	400+	700+	900+	1300+
STANDARD	25W	40W	60W	75W	100W
HALOGEN	18W	28W	42W	53W	70W
CFL	6W	9W	12W	15W	20W
LED	4W	6W	10W	13W	18W

Brightness in lumens vs. wattage is identified in different lamp types.

requirements and the diode's physical size and quantity, as selected by the manufacturer.

Also note that when LEDs were first introduced, bulb bases were huge! So, not only was each bulb and its cluster of nodes visible, glowing within the envelope of the bulb, but beneath it—right above the socket—was a large base designed to hide those components. Advances in microtechnology have shrunk those components. Now they are fully contained within the base and out of sight.

Unlike incandescent and halogen bulbs capable of delivering narrow beams of light outward, LEDs focus light in just one direction, upward. Thus they don't work well with reflectors. Underneath each node is the silicon material and heat sink, which the emitted light has no way of reflecting, as an incandescent PAR lamp or halogen MR-16 would do. What LEDs require, then, are optics that control the light after the node dispenses it. Modern automobile headlights and other high-quality products have extremely thick lenses or optics that funnel light through a thick layer of glass or plastic, much like a camera or microscope.

The design of optics for LEDs has just begun. In time, not having reflectors will no longer be an LED disadvantage, because there will be plenty of optics to act as substitutes. Along with optics come diffusers, which attach to fixtures to disperse and soften the flow of light. Like any other light source, LED diodes emit pinpoints of light that inevitably create glare, underscoring a need to diffuse the light they project. You really don't want to look directly at an LED diode. So, when dealing with LED "filament" bulbs, which loosely resemble the original Edison-invented filament lamps, make sure the light they project is tempered a bit.

When using strip or tape lighting to illuminate bookcases and countertops from above, installing a good diffuser over an LED strip achieves the effect of clustering the diodes together, so that light is projected evenly. Linear lighting applications are a major plus, because LEDs work so effectively in series—arranged in sequence, one after the other, and affixed to a flexible tape. These LED tapes function best when installed along cove moldings, in tray ceilings, and under cabinets. Without a good diffuser to disperse their light, however, LEDs will mirror the line of diodes in an unsightly way when focused on a lacquered ceiling or a shiny countertop. That's why it's extremely important to specify diffusers when ordering LED strip lighting.

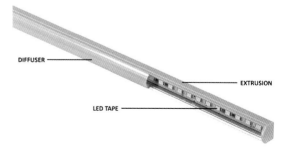

LED tape can be inserted into an extrusion to protect it from the elements, to provide a seamless installation, and to provide a way to attach a diffuser to focus the light and blend the diodes into a continuous linear strip of light. *Photo courtesy of Jesco Lighting*

Good-quality integral LED fixtures offer a good diffusion of LED light. Such fixtures have become more attractive from every viewing angle, and you won't see the "points of light" emitted by individual diodes. When integrating diffused LED strip lighting into your architectural millwork or cabinetry, take care to place each fixture inconspicuously, because there is nothing worse than a visible light source in a situation where the light has been designed to be indirect. A professional-looking result will keep the fixtures out of sight, layered behind good diffusers.

LEDs' only other disadvantage is that dimming them requires compatibility between the dimmer and the driver that powers them. That's why the traditional magnetic (autotransformer) dimmer, which would put resistance on the circuit to dim the incandescents, will not be effective with LEDs. Dimming is also referred to as "controls." While there are different ways to dim LEDs, it is important to consult the manufacturer's spec sheets, which offer compatible driver options.

Because the success of an LEDs, beyond the quality of its design, lies in its programming, only its manufacturer can be expected to advise how to dim it properly. Investigation will reveal that some companies market a broad range of products designed to successfully control most of the widely available LED bulbs.

Expanding Advantages

As LEDs have evolved, so have their methods of control. The greatest advantage of LED design is how well they integrate with the circuit boards that control them. Note that their output level can be manipulated when they are turned on. And they can be linked to so-called phototropic sensors that allow them to turn on and off automatically, depending on the amount of available daylight. Or, they can be linked to motion sensors that alert them to turn on when someone enters the room or the property. More and more smartphone apps are establishing links with electronic systems that "know" when your phone is active.

LEDs are low voltage—what does that mean? Since they use comparatively little electricity and "speak the language" of the circuit board, they lend themselves to programming. That means they can be turned on and off by such control systems as Iris, Vantage, Creston, Lutron, or Savant, among others. The control-system keypads are empowered to function beyond what you may think of when activating traditional "switches."

For example, these new controls may have six or more buttons that can be preprogrammed to render a variety of lighting moods. They do so by combining different lights that come on at different levels and in different color combinations to achieve specific effects. A case in point is the six-button control from Lutron, which eliminates a whole bank of switches, thus creating a cleaner interior elevation. And among the so-called "mood" settings will be ones that accommodate overcast days, dusk, evening entertainment, movie background lighting, or late-night intimacy.

The latest high-end touchscreen keypads are more intuitive and deliver a more satisfying user experience, such as using a tablet or smartphone to control not only the lighting but also music, temperature, window treatments, and security systems. The same motion sensors that turn lights on and off automatically can also activate an alert system when you're away from home, so that security lighting can be maintained without using energy needlessly.

LED use has spawned the development of myriad new technological products and services that will not only enhance your life at home but also ensure optimum energy conservation and peace of mind when you're away. We no longer have to wonder, "Did I turn those lights off?" or "Did I lower the thermostat before going on vacation?" Such technology, accessed from a smartphone or tablet, has spawned the term "smart home" and increased the value of a property, whether it's an apartment or a single-family residence.

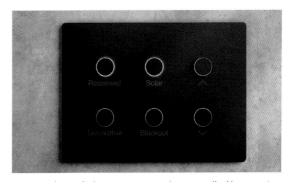

An entire home lighting system can be controlled by pressing buttons on a discreetly mounted keypad. *Photo courtesy of Lutron Electronics Co.*

LUTRON

Who wouldn't want to simply press an "All Off" button and have the temperature drop and every light switch snap off when you're about to leave your home? Or to activate certain functions when you're heading home so the house feels welcoming when you arrive.

It should be clear that a trinode LED is a color-change enabler. Clustering red, blue, and green diodes (RGBs) into a single trinode allows an LED light source to render millions of different tones just by altering the relative intensities of those three colors.

In-home control systems are localized. Known as DMX controllers, they can be accessed by a switch on the wall; thus their color and output are easily adjusted. Also, leading brands offer a variety of lighting-control systems capable of saving whole programming sequences. They can create scenic programming nodes that, if you wish, can simulate a nightclub effect or add some other dash of personality to your environment. Consider installing color-changing LED bulbs (RGBs) and light strips in areas of your home where you host guests. Even the remote controls offered by smartphone makers, and their apps, allow users to control color-changing LEDs in ways that are downright entertaining.

Recessed LED lighting has facilitated easier residential installation because the cans mounted within a ceiling's plenum space have become shallower. Because an LED is a diode affixed to a thin silica wafer, with only a heat sink behind it, an entire recessed-light housing may be as shallow as 2 or 3 inches, provided it has well-designed, low-profile optics. At one time, home builders had to make ceilings quite low to accommodate housings for recessed incandescent or halogen lighting, given the amount of heat they generated and the size of the lamping. Today's shallow recessed LED lighting makes it possible to build notably higher ceilings, which can greatly enhance interior aesthetics.

Recycling

What do you do with LEDs once they reach their end of life, or when a remodeling project mandates removing them? The answer: careful handling, even though one of their greatest attributes is their lack of toxic content.

Do not throw LED products in the trash. Just as LEDs can help us reduce energy consumption, it is our duty as respectful consumers to keep LED components circulating by recycling them. Since their makeup includes electronic gear along with plastic and glass, LEDs are certainly recyclable. Metal components within LED circuit boards contain copper and aluminum, which are the most-salvageable elements. Others, such as gold and nickel, believe it or not, can be recovered and extracted through the process of smelting, once you've disposed of the products. Separate LED waste according to how your community mandates the disposal of electronics.

Bulk waste disposal is a different challenge. If you're trashing an entire installation or a large commercial office space, companies such as NLR are equipped to deal with the bulk waste of all LEDs and their related components.

www.nlr-green.com

SAVE THE PLANET

Use energy wisely · Plant a tree · Use LEDs · Recycle

Super Control

The ease and efficiency of controlling them is one of the strong suits of LEDs. Since they are solid-state products, they operate in tandem with circuit boards, their actions directed by computer technology, which lends itself to programming. This accords us endless options for saving energy and also for expanding our ability to enjoy enhanced comfort and convenience at home.

Knowing how much lighting control you want will help you decide which products to bring into your home, starting with lightbulbs—or, as the industry labels them, LED retrofit lamps—which replace everyday household lightbulbs. Their brightness can be controlled by installing a wall-mounted dimmer. Manufacturers such as Lutron and Leviton market electronic low-voltage dimmers (ELVs) that work with most of the LEDs being sold today. Many of these advanced dimmers can also be accessed remotely, enabling you to turn circuits on before you get home or for security at night. A good rule of thumb: stick with the brands you're familiar with and trust.

LED retrofit lamp bulbs also offer tunability, which requires a control interface. I suggest consulting product literature, then downloading smartphone apps that allow you to tailor a lightbulb's color temperature to your liking.

Consummate Energy Savers

Clearly, the most significant outcome made possible by LEDs is energy saving. We've already discussed how LEDs can be activated remotely by motion sensors and occupancy sensors. They go on and off in response to movement and thus are on only when needed. In addition, programming lights to glow at less than full brightness can save a considerable amount of energy while creating a softer ambience when bright lighting is not needed.

There are ways to interface with your smartphone apps and take data from your GPS tracking system to activate lights as you approach your home, or deactivate them when you depart. My favorite is the smart home "All Off" feature, which, as mentioned, allows you to turn off every light in your home from your keypad or smartphone, after you've left!

In this book, I've intentionally left out much of the technical minutia that may simply confuse readers. Instead, I'll leave it to the professionals you may engage to upgrade your home's lighting system. Dimming alone has its complexities, for example, and there is more than one type, each with its particular benefits and drawbacks.

Some forms of dimming—pulse dimming, for example—send power on and off repeatedly. This happens so quickly, in fact, that the human eye doesn't perceive the light as either on or off but as just dim. Here are other examples:

- 0–10-volt dimming has universal appeal but requires installing an extra control wire between dimmer and driver.
- Trailing-edge dimming can operate without an extra control wire and is the most common form of ELV dimming.
- Leading-edge dimming, which was used with incandescents and halogens controlled by magnetic transformers, will not work with LEDs. They will cause flickering and cause LED diodes to burn out.

The reality is that in this fast-changing world of ours, many finite lighting issues can be left to certified electricians and lighting consultants. They are qualified to provide LED home lighting solutions that are game changers for your lifestyle and rewarding for your wallet.

So, what spate of innovations will be coming to market in the years ahead? One technology my firm looks forward to using more is organic LEDs, known as OLEDs, discussed in chapter 1. OLEDs allow thin, flexible materials such as textiles and wall coverings to become luminescent, creating exciting design possibilities. So much for the idea of illumination having to accommodate a hot, fragile, ephemeral Edison bulb.

For the sake of nostalgia, maybe we should hold on to our traditional lamps. In the future, instead of replacing the bulbs, we'll simply replace the old lampshades with new ones that light up!

An OLED chandelier called Versailles by Alexandre Boucher hangs in the Hall of Mirrors at Versailles, exemplifying the advancement in lighting over the past few centuries.

The Future of Light and Wellness

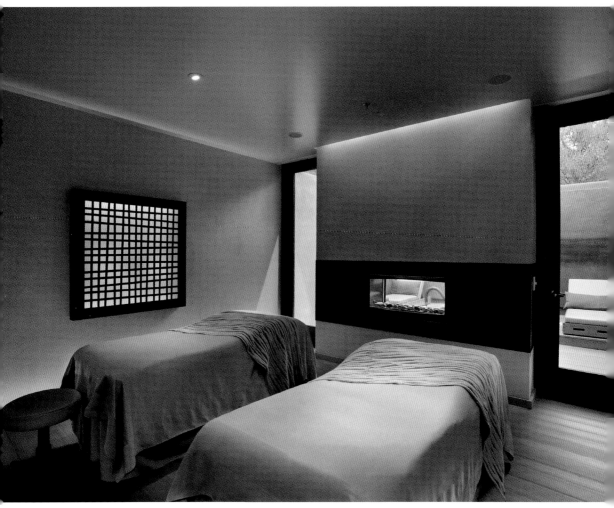

In a custom-designed massage room, LED lighting fosters an aura of serenity, aiding the user's perception of wellness. Design by Clodagh.

Depending on its color, light has a healing quality and can adjust to and support human circadian rhythms.

A sunlight substitute. We now know that it's not only the sun's rays that have the capacity to promote healthful sleep cycles. The use of artificial light can substitute for sunlight, as long as natural variations in color temperature occur throughout the day. This is known as human-centric lighting, a technology that's been fully recognized and practiced only in the twenty-first century but is not a new concept. Given the healing benefits of a consistent sleep cycle that supports our bodies' natural circadian rhythms, this technology has been used in hospitals and healthcare facilities for some time.

Many hospital patients endure insomnia resulting from limited sun exposure, pain, and treatment regimens. For one reason or another, their bodies have difficulty sustaining the circadian rhythm. And it's not just the hospitalized who suffer from chronic sleep deprivation. Spas and resorts are also incorporating human-centric lighting into their buildings to promote circadian rhythms. Now the manufacturers of these lighting systems are making their products widely available for residential use.

Philips Hues are just one example of tunable-white products that are easy to use and are designed to support any type of regimen you may wish to experience in your home. Such products will be particularly effective for folks on reverse work shifts, not just those looking to burn bright colors for a party. In time, more and more indirect-lighting products, such as those

During a soothing massage, color-changing LED lights by KETRA can influence the body's ability to relax and heal. When adjusted through a sophisticated system, lighting can not only address body ailments but also temper emotional stress. Design by Pavarini Design, Inc. *Photograph: © Marco Ricca Studio*

When considering our bodies' ability to heal, circadian rhythm is just the proverbial tip of the iceberg. As LED technology continues to evolve, the field of study known as chromotherapy has garnered new **attention in recent times.** Chromotherapy involves using the visible spectrum of colored light to heal physical, mental, and spiritual energy imbalance. This, too, is by no means a new field of study.

In constructing their temples, the ancient Egyptians incorporated colorful precious stones such as rubies and sapphires that, when sunlit from above, bathe people in red or blue light. The sick were literally "color diagnosed," and then dispatched to these red- and blue-light-washed chambers for healing. On a more spiritual level, some ancient Chinese cultures embraced color as a form of cosmic energy, or Chi, which can impact human energy and destiny.

The Greeks, too, were believers, recognized for having practiced solar therapy in Heliopolis, as the City of the Sun was known.

The rise of chromotherapy. With the advent of LED technology, chromotherapy is being taken to even-greater heights as a healing modality. These treatments range from laser puncture, where light beams replace needles, to light therapy,

known as Ketra, from Lutron, will bring refined ambience to the home, and new human-centric lighting alternatives will help people in all walks of life to experience healthful, balanced lifestyles with the help of color and light.

conducted to treat depression caused by seasonal-affective disorder (SAD). Laser therapy, prescribed to eradicate scars and stimulate living tissue, is often used as a non-invasive skin treatment for acne, sun damage, wound care, and other skin problems. This is just the beginning. Recently I've begun seeing advertisements for a type of head covering you can wear to stimulate hair follicles, purportedly to reverse baldness!

Color itself has been proven to have specific effects on the body and mind. Because color photons have their own wavelength and frequency, they can charge our cells in different ways to deliver the energy that manifests creativity, motivation, and happiness. We also know that color can relax the body, clear the mind of anxiety, and help rid us of enough stress to enjoy a good night's rest.

SCAN

CODE

PHILIPS

A juice bar, common in many custom-designed exercise and meditation rooms, includes a shelf for crystals and glassware; it is lit by an LED tape light tucked within the bracket. Design by Pavarini Design, Inc. *Photograph © Marco Ricca Studio*

Red, for example, has helped eradicate scarring, reverse signs of aging, and act on skin cells responsible for collagen production to reduce inflammation. Blue reduces the activity in sebaceous glands that produce oil; hence its use in reducing symptoms of acne by killing the bacteria that cause the inflammation.

Even smartphones and tablets have human-centric settings. They dim your screen as the day progresses and produce lower kelvin temperatures, thus aiding in the production of drowsiness-inducing melatonin at night.

Looking beyond circadian rhythm, researchers and doctors are embracing chromotherapy, having discovered that human metabolism is connected to circadian rhythms through the regulation of blood sugar and cholesterol. Can you imagine living in a modern home and not having to suffer from stress, lack of sleep, and other ailments as a result of your sophisticated home lighting system?

I'm in!

A Glossary of Common Lighting Terms

accent lighting: Directional lighting focused to draw attention to a particular object or field of vision

ADA wall brackets: Wall-mounted fixtures that extend less than 4 inches from a wall, in compliance with the Americans with Disabilities Act

alabaster: Like marble, a quarried stone that can be cut and adapted in different ways and also a popular, though costly, choice in crafting lampshades

alternating current (AC): The flow of electrical current delivered to homes and businesses; it reverses direction of flow multiple times per second.

ambient lighting: The background or fill light that illuminates a space

AMPs or amperes: The unit that measures the flow of electric current

architectural lighting: Built-in fixtures, such as downlighting or valance lighting, that are integrated into the architecture of a space

argon: An inert gas found in fluorescent and incandescent lightbulbs

average rated life: A rating, in hours, based on when 50 percent of a large group of lamps has failed

backlighting: Used to light stage sets, it creates subtle, indirect lighting on walls and other surfaces.

baffle: A translucent or opaque element that shields a source of light from direct view

bearing wall: A wall that provides structural support to ceiling joists and roofing elements

candela: A unit of measurement that records the intensity of light from a specific direction

candlepower: The intensity of light, as expressed in candelas

cans: A popular term for incandescent recessed downlights

casing: Trim that lines the inside and outside surface of a window frame or doorway

caulking: A waterproof adhesive filler flexible enough not to flake or pop out of cracks or seams

channel: A group of light fixtures that are operated together, their light levels either raised or lowered to achieve a particular effect

chromotherapy: Sometimes called color therapy or colorology, it is an alternative medicine method that is considered pseudoscience. Chromotherapists claim to be able to use light in the form of color to balance "energy" lacking from a person's body, whether on a physical, emotional, spiritual, or mental level.

circadian rhythms: These are twenty-four-hour cycles that help us carry out essential functions and processes. When synchronized with our brain's so-called master clock, circadian rhythms are directly influenced by such environmental cues as light, which, when cued appropriately, can promote restorative sleep.

circuit: A lighting path for the flow of electricity

circuit breaker: A safety device that can be set to prevent a possible excess flow of electrical current

cold cathode lamp: A specialty fluorescent whose unique construction, longevity, and custom-shape potential make it an ideal supplier of continuous indirect lighting. The "cold" label refers to the bulb's electrode, which functions at a cooler temperature than traditional fluorescents.

color-rendering index (CRI): A measurement of the ability of a light source to accurately render a color comparable to that issued by a natural light source, the sun

color temperature: Noted not in wattage but in degrees of kelvin (K), it measures the warmth or coolness of a particular light source. Kelvin temperatures for most lighting installations fall between 2,000K and 6500K.

compact fluorescent (CFL): A popular alternative to incandescent lighting, it burns up to ten times longer and is four times brighter than comparable incandescent bulbs.

cone reflector: A parabola-shaped device that eliminates brightness at high angles by focusing light directly downward

contrast: The difference in brightness between an object and its background

control system: A network-based lighting system controlled by one or more central computing devices

cove lighting: A light source that, when shielded by a ledge or other horizontal recess, can distribute light on a ceiling or upper wall

diffuser: A control device made of paper, plastic, fabric, or etched glass—each of which can be employed as a diffuser

dimmer: A control device that can raise or reduce the electric current flowing to a light source, thus varying the output of that light

dimming ballast: When teamed with a dimmer control, this special fluorescent-lamp ballast makes it possible to vary the light output.

direct current (DC): Electricity flowing continuously, in one direction, from positive to negative

DMX controller: DMX being an initialism for Digital Multiplex, this is the standard digital communication protocol used for controlling light fixtures.

dormer: A window installed upright in a sloping roof; also, the roofed projection in which the window is set

downlighting: The most direct form of top-down illumination, it casts light beams downward from an overhead fixture.

drywall (GWB): A wall-surfacing material composed of sheets of plasterboard or gypsum board known by the trade name Sheetrock. Also known as gypsum wall board.

efficacy (luminous efficacy): A measure of how well a light source produces visible light. It is the ratio of luminous flux to power, measured in lumens per watt in the International System of Units (SI).

electroluminescence: An electrical and optical phenomenon that emits light beams in response to a strong electric field or to the flow of electric current

electronic low voltage (ELV): ELV dimmers are also called simply "electronic dimmers" or "trailing-edge dimmers." These labels reflect the way in which this dimmer transitions your LEDs' luminosity. An ELV dimmer works like this: the electrical load is turned off at the end, or trailing edge, of the alternating current (AC) waveform.

Energy Star: An official US Environmental Protection Agency (EPA) designation assigned to products that meet strict energy-efficiency standards and thus have earned the right to be recognized, labeled, and promoted as Energy Star winners

extended-life lamps: Incandescent lightbulbs whose average rated life is 2,500 or more hours, compared to conventional incandescents (750 to 2,000 hours)

eyeball: An adjustable recessed accent-light fixture that extends slightly below the level of the ceiling

filament: The tightly coiled tungsten wire that is sealed within each lightbulb and glows when electricity flows through it

fill light: Illumination installed to expand the range of contrast or reduce shadows

finial: A decorative lampshade cap whose threaded interior enables it to be screwed into the top of a harp and secure a shade to a lamp

floodlighting: A system conceived to light an outdoor setting or object; its luminescence is greater than that of its surroundings.

fluorescent light: A low-pressure mercury-vapor gas-discharge bulb that produces short-wave ultraviolet light, which then causes a phosphor coating on the lamp's inner coating to glow. Light output far exceeds a comparable incandescent unit's overall efficiency. Fluorescent lighting products contain mercury and must be disposed of according to environmental regulations.

footlights: A set of strip lights mounted along the lower edge of a stage platform to add illumination and also offset face shadows produced by overhead lighting

furring: Strips of wood attached to a wall to provide framing support or create attachment points for hardwood paneling

glare: An annoying visual sensation brought about by lighting that is substantially brighter than that which dominates a particular field of vision

grounding: A method of safely connecting electrical elements to the earth

halogen lamp: Basically an incandescent light (lamp) within a quartz capsule filled with halogen gas. The result: a higher internal temperature and brighter, longer lamp life than is achieved by ordinary incandescent lights.

hard-back: This identifies a shade with a plastic liner.

harp: A shaped metal device used to attach a lamp to a shade

header: A structural support that forms the top of a doorframe, window, skylight, or other opening

human-centric lighting: A system that, where installed, will automatically change the color temperature of a space repeatedly throughout the day, transitioning from bright and energizing to warm and cozy, then back again

incandescent lamp: A device vacuum-sealed within a glass bulb in a vacuum that can produce light when a prescribed filament is heated enough by an electric current to produce light

indirect: A light source that directs light beams upward, then bounces them downward, supplying illumination with minimal glare, eliminating shadow

jamb: An upright piece or surface that forms the side of a door or window opening

joist: One of a series of parallel framing members that support a floor or ceiling load

kelvin (K): The Standard International (SI) unit of thermodynamic temperature that is now the specified unit of determining the global measurement of artificial lighting's newest forms

kilowatt: A measure of electrical power; 1 kilowatt equals 1,000 watts.

kilowatt-hour (KWH): A measure of electrical energy equivalent to the power consumption of 1,000 watts per hour

knee wall: A short, often non-weight-bearing wall that extends from floor level to the underside of rafters

LED: A light-emitting diode is a semiconductor device that converts electrical energy into light, directly and efficiently, with little wasted electricity.

LED driver: An electronic device that converts power input into an even and unvarying flow of electricity, thus compensating for fluctuating voltage

lens: A device used in light fixtures to direct or redirect illumination

load-bearing wall: A wall that supports the structure that rests on it by conducting its weight down to the foundation

louvers: An arrangement of baffles installed to absorb or deflect unwanted light beams

luminaire: A lighting device that comprises a lamp and its housing plus a reflector and a ballast

melatonin: A hormone your brain makes naturally to control your sleep cycle, it relates to the amount of light around you. Your melatonin level usually rises after sunset and remains high all night, dropping in the early morning to help you wake up.

miter: A joint in which the ends of two pieces of wood are cut at equal angles—usually 45 degrees—to form a corner

molding: A thin strip of wood whose profile is created by cutting and shaping

nonbearing wall: An interior wall that provides no structural support to any part of the house or building above it

OLED (organic light-emitting diode): A diode enhanced to include a filmlike layer of organic semiconductor material that emits light in response to an electrical current. The result: brighter, crisper light output using less electric power than conventional LEDs.

optoelectronics: The application and study of electronic devices that source, detect, and control the flow of light

OSB (oriented strand board): Made mostly of large wood chunks and pieces glued together, OSB is commonly used as a subflooring base because of its stability. The standard board size is 4 by 8 inches, its thickness varying from ½ to 1¼ inches.

particleboard: Made of wood dust plus small wood chips and particles, it is often called fiberboard and used as an addition to regular subflooring in wall-to-wall carpet installations.

partition wall: A wall that only divides space and is not weight bearing.

photometrics: Photometry is the science of the measurement of light, in terms of its perceived brightness to the human eye.

photon: The basic unit of all light, a photon is the smallest possible quantum of electromagnetic radiation.

phototropic sensors: A means of measuring how the presence or absence of light affects the growth patterns of plants and other organisms. Movement toward a light source is positive phototropism; growth away from light, negative.

plenum space: an area located between a building's structural ceiling and dropped ceiling that can be used to circulate heating, cooling, or return-air-flow systems

plywood: Wood slabs formed by three or more glued layers of veneer sold in sheets 4 feet wide by 8 feet long

power feed: A connection point from which electricity is delivered; it does not add to a structure's stability.

prism: A transparent plastic or glass refractor that has three or more straight sides and the capacity to bend light entering one side as it moves to exit another

rabbet: An L-shaped groove cut into the edge of a board, so it can receive the edge of another board

rafters: Wood boards installed to support a structure's sloping roof

RCP (reflected ceiling plan): A type of architectural drawing that provides key information about a room—dimensions, materials, and the orientation of various electrical or mechanical objects within the ceiling—as though you were positioned on the floor looking directly up

reflection: Diffuse light that bounces off a surface in all directions simultaneously

reflector: A device that redirects light flowing from a particular source

refraction: A process by which a ray of light changes direction as it passes from one medium to another

remote: An electronic device used or mounted separately from a dimmer; it can be operated from multiple locations, its light switched on at any desired dimming level.

retrofit: To upgrade room lighting by replacing lighting-system parts, equipment, or the fixtures themselves

ridge: The horizontal line at which two sloping roof planes meet and are joined

ridge board: The horizontal framing piece to which rafters attach at the roofline

riser: A vertical stair component that rises between treads

rough-in: Identifying probable lighting locations and installing essential electrical devices, after wiring a home and before doing the finish work

sconce: A bracket supporting an exposed or decorative wall-mounted light source

sheathing: The usually plywood exterior wall covering against which a brick, shingle, or stucco outer surface is applied

shim: A thin wood insert used to adjust the spacing between a floor and the sleeper laid over it

silhouetting: Accent lighting that achieves a dramatic outline through skillful use of backlighting

sleeper: In new floor construction, a strip of wood, usually a 2 × 4, laid flat over a concrete slab. A sleeper provides a base to which wood subflooring is fastened before a top layer of hardwood, laminate, or carpeting is installed.

soffit: The underside of an overhead architectural component—arch, balcony, beam, or balcony—that extends below a flat ceiling plane

solid-state lighting (SSL): A lighting form that employs LEDs, OLEDs, or polymer light-emitting diodes (PLEDs), rather than electrical filaments, to produce illumination

spider: The metal cross-frame at or near the top of a traditional lampshade

stringers: Diagonal boards, usually placed one on each side and one in the middle, to support stair treads

studs: Vertical components that when placed at each end of a wall and every 16 inches, on center, provide structural framing

subfloor: Made of plywood or a comparable sheet material, it is usually laid just before a finished floor is installed.

surface-mounted luminaire: A light fixture mounted directly on a ceiling

suspended luminaire: A light pendant hung from a ceiling by vertical supports.

task lighting: Illumination focused on a specific area where tasks requiring good visual acuity are taking place

three-way lamps: Incandescent lights with separately switched filaments that provide three wattage levels of light, as needed: 30/70/100, 50/100/150, or 100/300/300 watts.

toenail: A means of joining two boards together by nailing through the end, or toe, and at an angle of one board, then into the face of another

torchiere: A floor lamp that directs all or most of its indirect light upward

track lighting: A highly flexible system comprising individual lights or light groupings that are mounted on a wall or ceiling to provide overall task or accent lighting

transformer: A device geared to raise or lower electric wattage

treads: Horizontal boards on stairs, supported by stringers

trim: Strips of finished wood that can be used alone or combined with molding

trusses: Rafters supported by crossbeams in a roof-framing system

ultraviolet light (UV): A type of electromagnetic radiation that creates summer tans and makes black-light posters glow. It comes from the sun and is transmitted in waves or particles at different frequencies and wavelengths.

underlayment: Sheets of hardwood, plywood, or particleboard placed over old floor covering or a smooth, even new subfloor

Underwriters Laboratories (UL): An independent organization whose responsibilities include testing the safety of electrical products. Products passing UL tests can be labeled and advertised as "UL Listed," a sought-after designation.

up-lighting: A light source directed upward to illuminate a ceiling surface or act as a source of indirect lighting

vapor barrier: Material used in construction to block the flow of moisture

visual field: The scope of what you see when you look straight ahead and your head and eyes remain immovably fixed

wall-wash lighting: The smooth, even distribution of light on a wall

xenon: Filled with a heavy, colorless, and relatively inert type of gas, xenon bulbs produce an intense white or bluish light by passing an electric current through ionized xenon gas at high pressure. Xenon lights last longer and use less energy than halogens, thus are favored by most car headlamp makers.

CONTRIBUTING DESIGNERS

CLIFFORD STARR
cliffordstarr.com

CAROLINE RINKER
O'Blaney Rinker Associates
oblaneyrinker.com

BURT GRANT
Metro Area Sales
metroltg.com

CLODAGH
Clodagh Design
clodagh.com

DAVID KLEINBERG
David Kleinberg Design Associates
www.dkda.com

MARTYN LAWRENCE BULLARD
Martyn Lawrence Bullard Design
martynlawrencebullard.com

CHARLES PAVARINI III
Pavarini Design, Inc.
pavarinidesign.com

SABRINA BALSKY
Sabrina Balsky Interior Design
sabrinainteriordesign.com

DRAKE/ANDERSON
Jamie Drake / Caleb Anderson
drakeanderson.com

BONNIE STEVES
BJS-Assoc. Interior Design
bjs-assoc.com

JUAN MONTOYA
Juan Montoya Design
juanmontoyadesign.com

FERNANDO PAPALE
BP Architects
bparchitecture.com

CLAUDIA LECCACORVI
Raven Inside Interior Design
raveninside.com

ROBERT A. M. STERN
Robert A. M. Stern Architects, LLP
ramsa.com

BENNETT LEIFER
Bennett Leifer Interiors
bennettleifer.com

FRANCES TOUMBAKARIS
Francis Interiors
francisinteriors.com

JENNIFER POST
Jennifer Post Design, Inc.
jenniferpostdesign.com

DAVID SCOTT
David Scott Interiors
www.davidscottinteriors.com

JOHN BARMAN
John Barman Inc. Design and Decoration
johnbarman.com

ALEXANDRE BOUCHER
alexandreboucherdesign.com

ACKNOWLEDGMENTS

Visual Truth lies in the structure of light.
—Richard Kelly, lighting designer, architect

So many people offered support in my endeavor to write a book on residential lighting. Everyone I mentioned it to or discussed it with, without exception, was encouraging and in favor of a book on this topic, given the need for understanding of emerging LED technology and the paucity of reference books on the subject. Their interest has empowered me to move forward on this subject that impacts everyone. Thanks to all for your encouragement and help in achieving this career goal.

Joe Boschetti's involvement made this book become a reality. When I looked for a publisher, which took many months of persistence, I was finally introduced to Joe Boschetti, a publisher in his own right. Joe immediately responded to the concept of the book and aligned us with Schiffer Publishing.

The International Furnishings and Design Association , through its New York chapter, has always been there for me as a member. They have given me opportunities to share my knowledge with their audience, which in part confirmed my feeling that residential lighting is something very few know much about yet need to understand, given the LED revolution in recent years.

I first met Joseph A. Rey-Barreau when I took his LED seminar a few years ago. It was an excellent seminar with good practical info yet not overly technical. It was so inspiring that it made me want to learn more so I could begin to organize my own initiative to publish a book.

Dan Blitzer was the first person I went to when thinking of writing this book. His keen insight made us rethink how to formulate and present the information in an interesting and informative way. Our meeting with Dan initiated an agenda and organizational structure for the book, which led us to sort the information as a reference tool, making it easy for anyone reading the book to target the relevant chapter for reference when taking on their own projects.

Burt Grant and his company, Metro Area Sales in Hicksville, New York, introduced me to sources that have provided us with relevant product lines and content, such as illustrations and diagrams to reinforce the text. Burt is an incredible rescource of great lighting products and was always willing to help in whatever way to make this book possible.

As a technical reviewer and contributer on behalf of Lutron, Manny Feris and his team helped us convey some of the more challenging and specialized content to ensure accuracy, and provided information to supplement the concepts we addressed. He and Lutron are one of the most influential and reliable sources for great LED products and information in North America.

What would I do without Rose Hittmeyer? I am grateful for her extensive research and assistance in organizing images, release forms, and the manuscript—and for creating the clever cartoons. She beautifully captured me with my red glasses and ever-present necktie! Oh how the memoji brings youth to my visage!

I could not have done this without the Maria Ruiz. She masterfully illustrated many of the diagrams in this book to make it all the more clear and precise. She is always a team player, and her work is so important in communicating to our audience.

The late Lana Lenar was my mentor and company lighting designer for many years. She lit my projects with a keen understanding of who I am and how I see as a designer, acknowledging my aesthetic and quest to use the latest lighting technologies. Working with Lana was always an education and always a positive experience.

Cliff Starr has always been an invaluable part of my lighting career. He introduced me to some of the best lighting manufacturers, which I repeatedly specify on projects. His help forging those connections has led to some of the most important partnerships of my career.

Cynthia Turner has been a true supporter of my work to communicate my vision as an interior designer with an eye for lighting.

Most of all, I want to acknowledge coauthor Mervyn Kaufman for approaching me at a Designers Lighting Forum meeting and suggesting that we write a book. My immediate response was "me?" Yes, he thought it would be interesting to write a book on lighting from the perspective of an interior designer. So, through many stops and starts, sickness, surgeries, pandemic, and work, many years were spent regathering ourselves and completing the book. Merv immediately knew how to capture my voice. His patience has been undying!

This book would not be possible without the intelligence and diligence of my partner, J. Randall Tarasuk. He has kept us organized and focused and has added a layer of insight that has allowed me to expound on my thoughts and ideas in ways that have made it all the more interesting, relevant, and succinct.

Many manufacturers and lighting companies supplied photos that help readers understand this complex topic. With their images, the manuscript has gained clarity. All designers, no matter what discipline, are visual people, and I trust their imagery provides a clearer understanding of lighting's many facets. Our desire to harness light to support and enhance our lives is a mission we all share.

Thank you to Designers Lighting Forum (DLFNY) for accepting an interior designer on your board and for teaching me the true value of understanding light, a continual learning process. The programs we coordinate and the LEDucation you host have made light more understandable to professionals.

I offer a deep thank-you to all the designers who responded with beautiful photographs that illustrated not only beautiful design but thoughtful lighting. Without their images, it would have been difficult to convey the power of creative lighting in residential interiors. I am grateful for the spectacular lighting installations from Bennett Leifer, Francis Toumbakaris, Sabrina Balsky, Jennifer Post, Martyn Lawrence Bullard, Drake / Anderson, David Kleinberg, Clodagh, Bonnie Steves, Caroline Rinker, David Scott, Claudia Leccacorvi, Juan Montoya, John Barman, Fernando Papale, and Robert A. M. Stern.

May your *light* shine bright beyond L-70, be long-lasting, and share all the colors of the rainbow!

—Charles Pavarini III

Charles Pavarini III has a BFA in architectural interior design. He studied product design under Massimo Vignelli at Harvard and Palladian architecture throughout Italy. Among 34 design awards, Charles won a LUMEN Award for his lighting sculpture *Falling Sticks*. For more than three decades he has served the Designers Lighting Forum of New York. Pavarini has taught for 10 years at the Parsons–New School of Design and created a CEU course, "The Fundamentals of LED Lighting for Designers," which he presents nationally. Pavarini partnered with Alora/Kuzco to design six lines of decorative lighting launched in 2021 at Lightovation. He maintains offices in NYC and Scottsdale, Arizona.

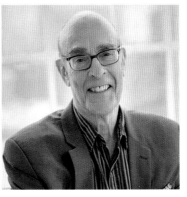

During a long publishing career, **Mervyn Kaufman**, former editorial director of *House Beautiful*, has edited home-themed special-interest magazines, written articles for home-interest publications, written nine nonfiction books for young readers, and authored five books on home design.

J. Randall Tarasuk, vice president of Pavarini Design, joined the firm in 1998 and since then has mounted some two dozen major design exhibitions, including six for the prestigious Kips Bay Decorator Show House. He has acquired an extensive knowledge of lighting technology and its applications.

00 5000 6000 7000